Praise for *Jock Talk*

"For anyone who wants to raise their game as a presenter or effective communicator, Beth Levine's 5 principles are spot-on! Beth's broad experience in coaching others coupled with great stories of athletes offers a refreshing set of insights from the field into the boardroom. A great read for all those who want to continue to master their voice and communications impact."

—AMY JEN SU, Co-Author, *Own the Room: Discover Your Signature Voice to Master Your Leadership Presence*

"As someone who has to speak publicly on a regular basis—but almost has a phobia of public speaking—Beth Levine has given me a sense of confidence in my own style and a focus on how to communicate effectively in a variety of settings. She presents her approaches and principles with humor that continually reminds me of ways to effectively deliver messages."

—MAYOR RALPH BECKER, Salt Lake City

"Beth simplifies a process that can be very intimidating for many people. Her guidance makes it easy to incorporate key messages when speaking to the media, large groups, or even co-workers on a daily basis."

—LINDA LUCHETTI, Executive Vice President of Communications, Utah Jazz

"Skill on the field or in the C-suite is no guarantee we can engage an audience or nail a media interview. Beth delivers razor-sharp insight for delivering a message in one's authentic voice. These simple principles work!"

—DEE BREWER, Marketing Executive,
The Taubman Company

"Thanks to Beth's media communications expertise, the next time I am unexpectedly confronted with a camera and a mic, I feel confident that I will be prepared to present our message with confidence."

—SARAH LEHMAN, CEO, Enve Composites

"Beth Levine knows her stuff! She's a communicator, trainer, and connoisseur of the written word. Sit back, relax, and let her take you on a wild ride to find your true voice."

—DAVE WENTZ, CEO, USANA Health Sciences

Jock Talk

Jock Talk

5 Communication Principles for
Leaders as Exemplified by
Legends of the Sports World

———◆———

BETH NOYMER LEVINE

SMARTMOUTH COMMUNICATIONS

GREENLEAF
BOOK GROUP PRESS

Published by Greenleaf Book Group Press
Austin, Texas
www.gbgpress.com

Distributed by Greenleaf Book Group

For ordering information or special discounts for bulk purchases, please
contact Greenleaf Book Group at PO Box 91869, Austin, TX 78709,
512.891.6100.

Design and composition by Greenleaf Book Group and Debbie Berne
Cover design by Greenleaf Book Group and Debbie Berne
Cover image: ©istockphoto/DNY59

Cataloging-in-Publication data is available.

ISBN 13: 978-1-62634-171-5

Part of the Tree Neutral® program, which offsets the number of
trees consumed in the production and printing of this book by
taking proactive steps, such as planting trees in direct proportion
to the number of trees used: www.treeneutral.com

TreeNeutral®

Printed in the United States of America on acid-free paper

15 16 17 18 19 20   10 9 8 7 6 5 4 3 2 1

Second Edition

*This book is dedicated to my father, Arthur Noymer,
an athlete and a gentleman; and to my mother,
Barbara Noymer, a prolific communicator.*

CONTENTS

Contents

FOREWORD

Thirty years ago I made one of the best business decisions of my career. I hired Beth Noymer Levine.

I had just started work in the world's largest PR firm, one of twenty-five people devoted full-time to a single Wall Street client. I was a mid-level member of the group, tasked with assembling a small team to promote our client's nascent investment banking business. Beth became part of our five-person investment banking communication team. It was 1985, the go-go years on Wall Street—just a few years before actor Charlie Sheen captured the pace and possibilities, as well as the consequences of overdoing it, in the film *Wall Street*. We spent our days at our client's Wall Street offices and trading floor, grazing for news by morning and early afternoon, and speaking with the *New York Times*, the *Wall Street Journal*, and other media by late afternoon, all to earn our client a disproportionate share of voice in the papers.

We were young and brash and somewhat fearless. We began not knowing a thing about Wall Street—in my job interview I had to point out that I didn't know the difference between a stock and a bond. My future boss reassured me, "you will." And indeed we learned. And Beth was a star, earning not only our trust but also that of our (sometimes difficult) client and the news media. She was very, very good at it.

After a few years, I left for another firm, and Beth also left for yet another. We reconnected at the end of the decade, when I became head of communication for a large investment bank. I retained Beth's firm. Beth became my advisor, and I discovered that she had assembled her own team of young, brash, and talented investment banking communicators.

A couple of years later I had begun teaching investor relations and financial communication at New York University's Marketing & Management Institute. They asked me to teach another course, so I needed to hand off Investor Relations. I could think of only one person to take over the course: Beth. She joined the NYU faculty and taught brilliantly for the next several years. Then her career led her to Atlanta, where she became head of corporate communications for a large bank—one that eventually would become part of Bank of America.

And then we went our separate ways. Beth started her own consulting practice and got involved in the world of Olympic and professional sports in addition to the corporate world. I spent the next twenty years building a crisis and leadership coaching practice, with a heavy emphasis on Wall Street, healthcare, and the military.

We reconnected over coffee in New York when she came to meet with people about her book idea—what became the book you are holding in your hands. And we discovered that we were each working on similar books—books on how to lead, build trust, and inspire loyalty through effective communication. Only

I was doing it through the metaphor of military strategy, she through sports. We didn't really compare notes. But we agreed to stay in touch.

My book came out in mid-2012; Beth read it only after she had finished writing hers. But—perhaps not surprisingly—the two books are completely aligned. We come at things from different directions and use different vocabulary. But we're fellow travelers, applying and interpreting the same principles in ways we have found to work for our clients. And why not? We came of age together, discovering the hard way what works and what doesn't. One small example: Beth's First Principle is audience-centricity. My book's Second Principle is that you can't move people unless you meet them where they are. Same idea. But hers also embodies her Fourth Principle: Brevity.

I was honored and humbled when Beth asked me to write this foreword. I devoured her book. It is brilliant. It is witty. And it works. I know that after you've read the book, and taken to heart Beth's principles and techniques, you will become a more effective communicator, and therefore a more effective leader.

Beth and I agree on this: If you cannot communicate effectively, you will not lead. Whether you're an athlete, a candidate for political office, a business executive, or just someone trying to build a career, you will benefit mightily from *Jock Talk*'s approach.

Onward . . .

Helio Fred Garcia
New York City, December 2014

Helio Fred Garcia is Executive Director of Logos Institute for Crisis Management & Executive Leadership and an Adjunct

Associate Professor of Management and Communication at New York University. He is author of, among other books, *The Power of Communication: Skills to Build Trust, Inspire Loyalty, and Lead Effectively* (FT Press, 2012).

PREFACE

Youth, they say, is wasted on the young—except perhaps when it comes to athletes. Young professional and world-class athletes have a sense of urgency, a drive to capture what they know won't be there for them in decades to come. In their on- and off-field performances, young athletes are called on to employ judgment and behavior that is older and wiser than their years. Many rise to the occasion; others don't. Nevertheless, their moments of genius and greatness come early, and there is much for the rest of us to learn from them.

Youth was indeed wasted on me, as I was privy to little sparks of history in the making without being fully aware of it at the time. When I flash back to the early 1980s and the start of my career, I now realize how close I was to people and events that were going to shape some of our twenty-first century realities.

My first colleague was Barack Obama. It was 1983, and we had both just graduated from college. We were hired as young editors at a New York consulting and publishing firm now owned by *The Economist*. Those were the days when Wang Computers dominated the word-processing market, and ashtrays were still a fixture in people's offices. Barack was just the guy at the next desk. So when reporters tracked me down during his first presidential campaign in 2008, I didn't have many stories to offer up. While we were friendly at the time, I hadn't paid close attention. It was our first job. Who knew he would become the leader of the free world? Certainly not I.

In my next two jobs, from the mid-1980s to the early 1990s, I worked as a PR flack on Wall Street. Bulge-bracket firms like Salomon Brothers, Merrill Lynch, First Boston, JP Morgan, Bank of New York—all of whom have since been swallowed up—were deal partners, clients, and/or coveted clients of the financial PR firms where I worked. I was assigned to write press releases, position papers, and speeches for early creators of mortgage-backed securities and for the innovators of derivative products like interest rate and currency swaps. These are the very financial instruments that grew up, got more and more sophisticated over the years, and eventually became the chief culprits in the demise of the American housing market and the breakdown of the economy in 2008. The people I wrote for at the time were some of the pioneers—brilliant visionaries of a new financial frontier—even though they spawned markets that most would argue spiraled out of control. Who knew that would happen? Certainly not I.

I went on to spin the communications for IPOs and for some of the earliest exchange-traded mutual funds, for hostile takeovers, and for their allegedly more genteel cousins, mergers and acquisitions, all of which required some fancy footwork with shareholder communications. I eventually became the head of corporate public relations for one of the predecessor banks of today's Bank of America. For public relations, investor relations, lobbying, proxy contests, sometimes for community and employee relations, and for a whole lot of media relations, I prepared the presentations as well as the executives who delivered them. It was a busy time, and I had a front-row seat, a keyboard, and fast fingers.

I developed a quick, easy rapport with the executives I prepped for their high-stakes communications, but I paid only as much attention to them and what they were doing as I needed to in order to do my job well. More than twenty years later, I can open *the Wall Street Journal* and other business publications and see the names and faces of the people I knew and worked with back then. Some reached the C-suite, and many have become legends in financial market folklore.

While I may not have been paying close attention to some things, here's what I *did* notice in those years: Business is complex. Messaging is key. Audiences crave and respond to simplicity. Sincerity meters are sensitive. Authenticity trumps slick and smooth every time. The high road beats the low road, hands down. Scrutiny is tough. Audiences are all-powerful. Well-prepared messages and messengers are in short supply.

Flash forward to the late 1990s. I had off-ramped from my corporate career to motherhood a few years earlier. I was now living in Atlanta and freelancing whenever old colleagues called for help in preparing their bosses and clients for presentations or encounters with the media. I was out for a walk one day, pushing child number two in a baby jogger, when the light bulb went on: This is its own niche business—preparing the messages and the messengers! It took a few years, but now the rest is history; SmartMouth Communications celebrates its tenth anniversary this year.

And messaging is still key.

Today everyone has a brand to build. Everyone's story is complex. Everyone's audience is discerning. After my Wall Street experiences, helping clients communicate complex stories to discerning audiences became second nature. I have CEO clients today who retain me as a consultant just to help think through complicated business issues and how they will play out with different stakeholders. I have clients who retain me to "channel" their voices and help develop a narrative that will be simple, that will resonate, and that will have impact. Helping clients to be "media ready" remains a favorite specialty. And I work with companies and organizations of all types to train client- and outward-facing employees to be better spokespeople and to give customers a better experience in meetings and presentations.

I love my work and my clients—and I am definitely on full alert now, I assure you. I attribute this in part to maturity, but also to feeling incredibly privileged to coach and consult with a diverse range of aspirational people and organizations that just might make history themselves someday. In addition to corporate executives and innovators, there are doctors, lawyers, entrepreneurs, nonprofit executives, political candidates, elected officials—and athletes. Athletes have captured my heart and my fascination. Often unfairly underestimated intellectually, they are uniformly smart, quick-thinking decision makers; they are intensely driven and mission-focused; and they so often have rich, inspiring life journeys and stories.

And athletes—because they inadvertently end up being society's public-speaking guinea pigs, heroes, and fallen heroes—are the teachers in this book. Why? I had an epiphany when I realized, shortly before addressing an NBA team on the topic of media relations, that in the span of a typical six-month season, a team will play eighty-two games and therefore there will be at least eighty-two turns at the microphone for several of the players. Eighty-two times in six months! That's more frequently than the president of the United States holds a press conference and far more frequently than most CEOs address any type of an audience. And no one on Wall Street speaks publicly that often—certainly not these days.

So, with a tip of the hat to all the rookie and veteran athletes out there, I present *Jock Talk* to the business community. I hope that it helps you find your voice, refine your message, and fulfill your professional aspirations.

Beth Noymer Levine
September 2014

GOING FOR GOLD

What is it about winning a gold medal that drives people to years of grueling training and conditioning despite the extremely low chances of ever standing on the podium? Why are there professional-level and world-class sporting events, some that pit people from different countries and even from different hemispheres against one another? What motivates people to work so hard and invest so much of themselves in athletic pursuits? Why aren't they satisfied to compete only recreationally and at a local level? *There is something about winning, about being the best— possibly the best in the world—that is hardwired into the human spirit.* It's just there. No matter what your field of play—sports, medicine, education, the arts, or business—you have very likely daydreamed about, if not actually strived for, being the very best at what you do.

Most leaders have imbued their organizations with this same drive to win and have put into place a training regimen to capture the gold. Consider these: *Mission. Values. Excellence. Accountability. Productivity. Efficiency.* Words like these are rightfully part of the lexicon of organizations that strive to rally their employees to achieve greatness. But too often an important word is missing in the pursuit of a winning performance or a world-class reputation: *Communication.* No one is making communication a part of the training regimen. That's probably because communicating is assumed to be something people just do, like breathing. Yet it's not.

I view communication as the everyday currency of business; it's how we get things done. Our success is ultimately determined by interactions with employees, customers, communities, suppliers, shareholders, regulators, and other stakeholders. And while most organizations have a mission statement, and many articulate a set of core values—for how they conduct their business or treat each other and their customers—most overlook standards, goals, or guidelines for communicating. Communication is actually the channel for executing a company's mission, its values, and its expectations for excellence, accountability, productivity and efficiency. How else could these be realized?

In a fascinating random sampling of the websites of twenty large, well-known companies—including Coca-Cola, General Electric, Amazon, Google, Samsung, FedEx, Starbucks, Southwest, Delta, Nike, American Express, Merck, Proctor & Gamble, IBM, Home Depot, LVMH, Fiat Chrysler, Bank of America, Microsoft, and DuPont—I found that only one explicitly addressed communication. Sixteen of these corporations are on *Fortune*'s "Most Admired Companies 2014" list, but it turns out that only Delta highlights communication, and does so repeatedly, in its "Rules of the Road"—a mission- and value-laden manifesto created under Delta's post-bankruptcy CEO Richard Anderson, who took the helm in 2007. Flash forward to 2014, and Delta is being lauded as the top-performing U.S. airline. An article in *The Street* even quoted an airline industry analyst who called Delta the "king of the jungle."[1] While it may be a stretch to attribute such success solely to Anderson's explicit directives regarding communication, they are quite likely contributing factors in Delta's winning game strategy.

Lean and Mean?

When it comes to how organizations communicate, I am struck by how corporate leaders strive for excellence and efficiencies in so many operational areas, yet are willing to settle for merely adequate—or worse, time-wasting—when it comes to business communications. Meetings, presentations, and speeches are so often where and how business gets done, but in these settings mediocrity abounds. Many companies in the manufacturing sector even subscribe to the tenets of the Lean Movement yet tolerate flab and time-wasting in communications.

The *Wall Street Journal* reported on the "Executive Time Use Project"[2]—a joint Harvard-London School of Economics study—which found that CEOs spend 45 percent of their time in meetings of some form, which only *begins* to capture how much time high-level executives spend communicating. The same study says that CEOs spend only 10 percent of their time working alone, which means that 90 percent of their work is accomplished in the presence of others—with interactions that surely demand verbal input from the leader. When you consider the amount of work time that all executives spend with others, effectiveness in communication is clearly an essential element of the success of both the leaders and their organizations.

A recent study in the *Journal of Marketing Communications* finds a causal link between communication effectiveness and economic performance. "Companies that align communication with the corporate mission and strategy score significantly better not only on 'soft' measures such as image and awareness but also on 'hard' economic measures, especially on relative market success in the industry."[3] In sum, the more effective a company is at communicating—internally and externally—the greater the company's general performance. Perhaps most telling, the *Journal* found that companies whose executives support improving communication, and recognize its economic value, performed better than companies without supportive leadership.

Amateur Hour

It's a reality that business communication is often delivered in presentations, most of which involve the ubiquitous PowerPoint. According to a report by *Bloomberg Businessweek*, "since Microsoft launched the slide show program 22 years ago, it's been installed on no fewer than 1 billion computers; an estimated 350 PowerPoint presentations are given each second across the globe; the software's users continue to prove that no field of human endeavor can defy its facility for reducing complexity and nuance to bullet points and big ideas to tacky clip art."[4] Yale professor (and noted PowerPoint critic) Edward Tufte concurs, adding that *"PowerPoint allows speakers to pretend that they are giving a real talk, and audiences to pretend that they are listening. This prankish conspiracy against evidence and thought should provoke the question, Why are we having this meeting?"*[5]

Prankish conspiracy indeed. Certainly, there are good PowerPoint presentations, too, but they seem to be the exception. Regardless, time is one of the scarcest and most valuable resources for all business people, yet management pays little attention to improving the biggest time-sink: communication in meetings and presentations. I am amazed at how few "pros" there are out there and how many organizations send out "amateurs" to lead and deliver important meetings and presentations. I've watched more than a few times as the executives in charge just close their eyes, hold their breath, and hope for the best. Sometimes, they get lucky, and the amateurs bring home a win; other times, they don't. That being said, there is most definitely room for companies to rethink how they communicate in order to reach the next level of excellence.

Raising the Bar

Tolerance of mediocrity in business communication is my pet peeve. It's not only the mediocrity itself that bothers me, it's also the acceptance of it and the lack of action taken to remedy it. There are simply too few people calling phooey, or if they are calling phooey, they don't know how to change things for the better—how to raise the bar.

I believe you can start with this: Make medal-worthy communication skills a core value. Then get to work on making them a core competency.

Organizations hire me to work one-on-one with executives or to train executive teams. Often they come to me with a wish list like this: *They're so long-winded, can you make them more succinct? Can you add some polish and professionalism? They need to make a better impression. Is there any way you can make them sound more commanding?* I can, and I usually do. Most of the time what they have been delivering, and how they have been delivering it, has been adequate—not particularly bad, not particularly good, simply adequate. It met the low standard that business audiences have come to expect.

Well, what is standard in the business world may be adequate, but it's not optimal and, let's face it, it shouldn't be acceptable. Think about how often you roll your eyes during meetings that are too long and, worse, pointless. Think about the boring presentations you've sat through—the ones in which you waited for the single valuable nugget, that one answer, that lone call to action that came at minute 52 out of an hour-long talk. Think about the speech by the CEO who was incredibly dry or who mouthed the same old-same old. A bar set at adequate or standard is far too low for organizations that expect excellent outcomes—or aim to be the best in the world.

One of the most challenging aspects of my work as a coach and trainer revolves around the fact that I'm in the business of asking people to change something about themselves or about how they typically conduct themselves. To make matters a little more challenging, I am asking them to alter *how they speak*—as if speaking in public weren't already unpopular enough. It's all too common for even the most high-achieving, high-potential types to see the podium as an obstacle to be avoided rather than embraced.

But there's really nothing to be afraid of; the podium—or the front of the room—is an advanced field of play that can be exploited to achieve excellence. All that's needed are the tools and the willingness to work at it. I remind clients to keep Michael Jordan's famous quote in mind: "I've missed more than 9,000 shots in my career. I've lost almost 300 games, and 26 times I've been trusted to take the game winning shot and missed. I've failed over and over and over again in my life. And that is why I succeed."

As a coach, I pride myself on being sympathetic—and even empathetic—with executives, as I, too, have public-speaking foibles that I work to improve. I reassure clients by letting them know I am not going to attempt to turn them into Cicero or Patrick Henry (both famous for their orations)—or even Muhammad Ali. Rather, I am going to get them to up their game. I want to help them become the best speakers and presenters they can be—one baby or giant step at a time, depending on their levels of motivation and readiness. I guide them toward discovering what they need in order to be better; for different people that means different strategies.

Still, there are some overarching strategies that everyone can embrace. The five principles in this book—and the proprietary presentation framework in the last chapter—have proven to be effective with all levels of management. More often than not, clients grasp the concepts quickly and prove they can put them into practice. I encourage you to read on and take some time to digest the ideas. Then, see what you can do to turn some or all of the five principles into a set of core communication values that demand excellence and enhance performance—yours and your organization's.

Communicating is not as effortless as breathing—just as placing in the 200-meter butterfly isn't as effortless as simply swimming. It requires focus, hard work, and the desire to master it. Excellence in communication needs to be an expressed organizational value, and it needs to be valued starting at the top. Only then can you and your team begin to see yourselves on the gold-medal podium.

CHAPTER 1

PRE-GAME PEP TALK

"You can do it!"

I have it all set up. The camera guy is looking through the lens of his TV studio camera, which is set on a tripod and fixed on the two chairs that face each other. The big-screen monitor for watching instant replays is next to the two chairs. The young NBA player walks into the room after practice. He has showered and dressed in his team sweats, and while everyone else has gone home for the afternoon, he has agreed to submit to some one-on-one media training in advance of what promises to be a busy season on the floor. He's barely a man in chronological age, but he's physically huge, at just under seven feet tall. We shake hands; he sits down. I ask him if he's ready to begin. He says he is.

The camera is rolling. I hand him an ordinary toothbrush. He looks at me, perplexed, clearly thinking, *This is not what I agreed to do for the next two hours.*

I ask him only a few questions about the toothbrush: What is that? What do you do with it? Do you like it? How often do you use it? What do you like about it?

He answers haltingly and offers simple, one-word responses.

Then we're done with the exercise. We watch the instant replay of his "toothbrush interview," and finally I explain the method behind my madness.

I do the toothbrush exercise with many of my clients, both athletes and executives. It is a defining and memorable exercise, and it is always totally unexpected . . . but not always well received, at least initially. After all, what does a toothbrush have to do with sports or, for that matter, with communicating?

Nothing. But it has everything to do with being able to think about your audience, be yourself, be nice, get to the point, and be prepared for all of the above, which is what the chapters in this book cover.

The lesson of the toothbrush exercise is that no matter how mundane, obvious, or self-explanatory the questions or issues are, you need to be prepared at all times to address your audience in a positive, sincere, and robust manner. And there's nothing more mundane, obvious, or self-explanatory to have to talk about than a toothbrush.

Why Athletes as Teachers?

Floor time. It's all about the floor time. When it comes to a career trajectory, executives, like athletes, often come up through the ranks by earning more and more floor or field time, demonstrating at each step of the way that they have the necessary competencies behind them and a ton of potential ahead. For executives, like athletes, the path is sprinkled, if not littered, with public speaking opportunities. Communication is the most basic currency of business and success—no one gets ahead without needing to speak or present in front of others. The persona you cultivate and project—the tone you strike, the voice you use, the attitudes you convey—can be career-makers or -breakers for athletes and executives alike.

When athletes speak or present, they are typically in front of the media, whether at a pre-game event or post-game interview, at a press conference, or on a talk show. These are high-stakes appearances; they're very public, and video clips live forever on the Internet. But then, of course, there are many more discreet occasions that are just as important, such as meetings with owners and sponsors, "fan touches," and community and celebrity events.

As an executive, your speaking engagements parallel many of those, but you are usually communicating to board members, employees, customers, industry peers, investors, analysts, and community and political leaders. At the end of the day, you, like a professional athlete, are responsible for building a franchise—by winning fans, fostering team and brand loyalty, motivating others, displaying and building team enthusiasm, behaving admirably in the spotlight, and handling public criticism and praise equally well.

I've written this book so that I can coach more people than I'm able to meet, and I want to start by telling you that you *can* be super effective in front of a group! Trust me when I say that no one is "a natural" at speaking and presenting; even the best of the best think about it and work at it. So whether you're pretty close to the pro level or still an amateur, you can adopt and adapt the basic tenets of this book and begin to move the dial on your performance, right away. It's not that hard. You can do it!

You're probably pretty darn good already. But if you've reached for this book—or if someone has given it to you—you probably care a lot about your professional presence and tone. This book will share five fundamental principles of communicating. It will give you the confidence to know that you're "doing it right," and it will give your audience the impression that you're an all-star.

Five-Star Approach

The five principles are:

- Audience-centricity
- Transparency
- Graciousness
- Brevity
- Preparedness

Taken together, they send two really important messages about you to your audience: 1) that you care about and respect them, and 2) that you're real and therefore credible and trustworthy.

Audience-centricity may be a new term to you, yet it's probably the most fundamental of the five principles. Simply put, audience-centricity is making the audience's interests and experience a top priority in the planning and execution of a talk. Too many speakers prepare and deliver what is important and interesting to themselves without enough careful consideration of their listeners. Being audience-centric is a mindset shift that encourages the speaker to prepare and deliver content in a way that will matter to and resonate with the audience.

Transparency is exactly what you think it is; it's about being open and direct—yes, and honest, too. Transparency is critical. It contributes to the levels of sincerity and trust that are accorded to you by your audience.

Graciousness is the art, skill, and willingness to be kind-hearted, fair, and polite. As motivators and influencers, love and peace work far better than hate and war. Speaking in positives rather than negatives leaves lasting, favorable impressions.

Brevity is a crowd-pleaser and needs no further introduction.

Preparedness speaks for itself as well, especially because the unprepared speaker is the one who is most likely to be long-winded—not to mention unfocused. While the mere thought of preparation might bring on feelings of dread or even impossibility, there are ways to prepare that take only seconds but that can greatly enhance a speaker's effectiveness.

What about practice? you might ask. Practice is great, obviously, and essential for an athlete. I'm a big advocate of practice, but I'm also a realist about time. The five principles in this book don't ask much of you in terms of a time commitment. What this book encourages you to do is think about what you say and how you say it, because with just a few subtle adjustments you can make some significant strides. As Yogi Berra said, "Baseball is 90 percent mental. The other half is physical." The same is true for speaking!

Interestingly enough, you already have what could be considered the home-court advantage: Audiences expect the best from you; they assume, when you get up to talk, that you'll succeed. So you already have that in your favor. The five principles in this book will give you that extra leg up; they will take you to the next level—where you are able to engage, connect, and be impactful.

The next five chapters open, as this one did, with real-life jock stories, followed by a discussion of how those stories illustrate the chapter's communication principle. As a recap and reinforcement, each chapter concludes with three practical takeaway tips for you. Following those, you'll find a practice exercise or a self-assessment, with prompts to help you, and space for answers and notes.

Success is in the eye of the beholder—your audience. *Jock Talk* will help you achieve a new level of success in everyone's eyes. Athletes do best when they give their physical all. Leaders do best when they give their emotional all. Show care and respect, be real, and your audience will listen and be impressed.

Pre-Game Pep Talk

The five-star approach to all-star public speaking—audience-centricity, transparency, graciousness, brevity, preparedness—requires three key elements:

1. **Consider your audience.** The basic mindset shift, the simple awareness, of striving to be more audience-centric than egocentric can significantly change how well you perform and how you are perceived.

2. **Be positive and sincere.** Your tone and style—and therefore your image and the image of your organization—can be dramatically improved by paying attention to how sincere and positive you are when you speak.

3. **Respect your audience; be prepared.** No one, especially not you, is more important than an audience; treat all your listeners with respect by preparing, even if only briefly, before you speak.

Practice Exercises

Try the toothbrush exercise with any ordinary household or personal object. It could be a toothbrush, a fork, a chair, even a hat or a newspaper. Describe the object. What is its use and significance? Where did you get it? Do you like it? Does it have any special meaning to you? Try to be positive, sincere, and energetic, and give full (but not too lengthy) answers. If it's easy and convenient, you could have a friend or family member use a cell phone to video your answers.

Once you've tried this with a household object, you might want to think about an aspect of your work or business that has become so rote or routine for you that you have lost touch with how to talk about it. Imagine that you're talking to a completely uninformed, uninitiated audience, and see if you can be clear and robust in your explanation. For example, what business are you in? What are you working on these days?

_____

_____

_____

_____

_____

_____

_____

_____

_____

_____

_____

_____

_____

_____

_____

_____

_____

_____

_____

_____

_____

_____

CHAPTER 2

PLAYING TO YOUR FANS

"It's all about them—it's not about you!"

Following his defeat by Roger Federer in the 2012 Wimbledon gentlemen's final, Andy Murray makes an emotionally raw concession speech. With his first words he congratulates Federer on the win. Then, as he struggles to compose himself and fans fill his pauses with cheers, he thanks them.

"Everybody always talks about the pressure of playing at Wimbledon, how tough it is, but it's not the people watching—they make it so much easier to play. The support has been incredible, so thank you."

By contrast, Michael Jordan, in his now notorious 2009 Basketball Hall of Fame induction speech, takes to the podium assuming that the audience will be on his side. His physical appearance is a surprise to those who haven't seen him since his playing days—he's thicker than the lean leaper most remember, as he's now middle-aged—but he is one of the greats, a venerable player who raised the bar for generations of players to come.

At the microphone to accept his long-anticipated and well-deserved honor, however, Jordan begins to ramble, rant, and riff on coaches and players he's known over the years. In story after story about himself and, frankly, about his superiority, he ends up displaying aspects of his personality less worship-worthy than his athletic achievements. Midway through his speech, he even tells his three children in the audience, "You guys have a heavy burden. I wouldn't want to be you guys if I had to, because of all the expectations you have to live with." Only in the final two minutes of his twenty-three-minute harangue does he refer to his note cards and deliver some thoughtful insights and valuable lessons from his years as a megastar.

An inclination to be an egocentric versus audience-centric speaker is as natural and common among business executives as it is among athletes and can manifest itself in many ways.

When you get up to talk or take the microphone at an event, it is not, and should not be, all about you—not if you want to be effective, impressive, and memorable, that is. There is an unwritten, unspoken contract with your audience that you, the speaker, will entertain, enlighten, or energize them. Personal stories need to support a point. The time you take needs to be used to deliver something of value. An audience waits for something new, useful, beneficial, or fun. Audiences, and certainly fans, like to be acknowledged somehow. In order to deliver on any or all of this, you must prepare your remarks with your audience's experience in mind. That is the essence of being audience-centric.

Audiences all have biases, self-interests, and expectations. They have a very basic "what's in it for me?" thread running through their subconscious. They want something in exchange for their time and attention. As if that weren't enough, they also don't want to work hard. Unless you guide them and tell them where you're taking them, they won't make the connections and get there on their own. To make matters slightly more challenging, competition for people's attention is tougher, and their devices—cell phones, laptops, tablets—are ubiquitous (although the presence of devices can also be a good thing, as increasingly people use them to take notes).

Finally, an audience sizes you up immediately and, within seconds, decides if you are worth their attention and engagement. There are studies showing that this happens in the first *eight seconds*. Think about that: In the first eight seconds, people decide whether to listen to you or not. This certainly puts some weight on how you open your talk.

All of this adds up to a tall order. It demands that you, the speaker, think about your audience more than just superficially. Your topic and your time allotment may be fixed, but your audience is a variable, and that should guide you in preparing what you deliver and how. The experience you give them will stay with them longer than any words or data you share.

Too many speakers and presenters—in fact, probably the very same ones you and I have complained about—clearly approach the podium without having given a minute of consideration to their audience's interests or concerns, or quite possibly even to whom their audience is. They simply deliver what's important or compelling to *them* about their topic. Perhaps you've listened to speakers who deliver canned presentations, without regard for the city they're in or the group they're in front of that day. That's an example of an egocentric speaker, and that person's inability to recognize or acknowledge, even indirectly, the audience's "what's in it for me?" causes him or her to lose big points.

What's at stake when the speaker skips over the audience's

sensitivities? There's a risk of losing credibility and likeability—two pretty strong desirables for a speaker. Ask yourself *What's probably on their minds?* or *Which aspect of my topic is most likely to resonate with them?* or *At the end of the day, what does this audience really care about?* That will be an enormous help to you in figuring out how to frame your remarks. Even simply speculating on what your audience might care about is better than ignoring it altogether.

In Andy Murray's case, he knew his fans were hurting almost as much as he was, and he decided to tip his hat to them. It was a very endearing moment. Conversely, Michael Jordan's fans may have placed more value on his big moment than he did and hoped to hear some higher-level reflections from one of the NBA's greatest, rather than the petty poking and jabbing they got instead. Jordan failed to consider the audience's experience, while Murray nailed it.

Here are a few egocentric behaviors that I bet you'll recognize:

- **When speakers are paralyzed by their own nervousness before speaking, it's all about them and not about the audience.** They're worried more about how they look and sound than whether they're actually connecting with the people sitting in front of them . . . so then they don't.
- **When speakers run over their allotted time, it's all about them and not about the audience.** Sometimes they get carried away. They're unconsciously (at least I hope it's unconscious!) assuming they're so smart, so interesting, and so witty that the audience loves the sound of their voice as much as they love talking. More often, though, it's the speakers' drive to be thorough or to get through their entire deck of slides

that causes them to run into overtime. Either way, the resulting TMI (too much information) effect shows a lack of regard for the audience's interests, time, or overall experience.

- **When speakers read their own PowerPoint slides off the screen, it's all about them and not about the audience.** They've developed the slides to be a script for their presentation rather than a visual aid for the audience. I always say that Microsoft named it PowerPoint, not EveryPoint, for a reason: It was intended to be a tool to help the audience understand and retain information, not to help the presenter to present.

- **When speakers figure they'll "wing it" and don't need to prepare ahead of time, it's all about them and not the audience.** Some may have bought into their own hype, thinking, *Gee, I was invited to be the speaker; I'm an expert on the subject matter; therefore anything I have to say will be compelling. The audience is lucky to hear from me.* But more often, it's just that these speakers feel they are simply too busy to prepare. Unfortunately, an audience can perceive this omission as arrogance or lack of genuine interest. Even a few minutes of prep can prevent leaving the wrong impression.

When you think about it, you've probably bristled at speakers and presenters who have exhibited some of the preceding behaviors, haven't you? We have a hard time giving away our precious time and TMI getting something for it. When you are the speaker or presenter, you need to have an acute awareness of your content, time, and delivery. A "do unto others as you would have them do unto you" mentality is one of the single best tools you can employ. It's the Golden Rule, the ethic of reciprocity, and it's applicable to speaking and presenting as much as anything else. In fact, the

Golden Rule should be universal; if it were, then most of today's business presentations and even meetings would be a lot more tolerable—perhaps even enjoyable!

Just as we speakers are, every audience is a ticking, "what's in it for me" time bomb, waiting for the useful, meaningful, or valuable nugget that a speaker has to offer. And all speakers face the "who's it all about" trap; their work, expertise, or personal experiences are the topic, but they have to meet their audience's needs and expectations. Spend a minute or two identifying what you have to say that is useful, meaningful, or valuable to an audience. That will be the ultimate alignment of speaker and audience self-interests. It requires a bit of forethought, but it has a big payoff when the audience leaves the room feeling considered and satisfied.

How Can I Make Sure I'm Audience-centric and Not Egocentric?

If you're wondering how you can check on your own audience-centricity, ask yourself this question and then let the answer help you in your planning and preparation: If an audience member is asked, "What did you think?" what would you want his or her answer to be?

As an example, when I deliver presentations or workshops at large conferences, my answer to that question would usually be: I want audience members to say, "Wow, I got some great insights and tips that I can put to use right away."

I could easily deliver a canned "Effective Communications" presentation to every audience, but I always customize. I know my expertise and my material, and I'm always eager to share it, but then I think about each particular audience's "what's in it for me?" and I adapt my approach and material accordingly. I always want them to feel that they got something they can use right away.

I have on occasion been asked to speak about myself and my career. Naturally, this stops me dead in my tracks. After all, it's not all about me, it's about them. So in addition to what I'd want them to think about my talk, I also ask myself, "What is it about me or my career that could be beneficial or significant to this particular audience? What can I leave them with that might be helpful to them?"

So how do you take a topic that is all about you (or your expertise, your business, or your project) and make it all about them?

Very simply, you need to do at least the first two of these three things.

First, *know your audience.* Even if you're just making an educated guess, identify your listeners' unique interests, concerns, or biases.

Second, *prioritize your content.* That means prioritize what you say to them and then prioritize how—in what order, in how much detail—you want to say it. Avoid TMI; that's presentation buzzkill.

Third, if you can, *pinpoint a takeaway*—a lesson, a moral of the story, a call to action. This is where some of those presentation catchphrases come in: "Have a big idea." "Give 'em the so-what." "Identify your wow." These slogans essentially refer to value. Given your topic, what do you have that's of value to offer to your audience?

I have a CEO client who started a fast-growing business in the digital marketing arena. When the company was still a young player in that space, he was invited to speak at two major industry conferences, both in Europe and both with global audiences. It was a coup to be given these platforms. He knew his company had a solution that every digital marketer needed, and he would have loved to expound on it, but he also knew he wasn't allowed to "sell" while speaking onstage.

I worked with him to develop his presentation so that he would educate and enlighten his audiences enough to leave them wanting to get in touch afterward. He could have opened by giving background on himself or what his company does. Instead, he used the first ten seconds to empathize with his audience's single greatest business challenge. He then walked them through some market insights and some lessons learned. Finally, he closed by tying it all back to the initial challenge. Mission accomplished! By sharing insights and lessons, he delivered a very beneficial "what's in it for me?" to his audiences, and conference attendees at both events swarmed him in the hallway after his talks. He was thrilled with the response, and after that, he was invited to present at several other major conferences.

Being audience-centric requires you to literally put yourself in someone else's shoes. Take a few minutes and try out these scenario exercises.

If I'm an employee, and I know the company has been struggling for several quarters, what would I want to hear the COO address in an all-hands meeting, and what do I want to hear first?

1. "Good morning. It's good to have you all assembled. Let me start this meeting by giving you a bit of historical perspective on our company and then an overview of the past year so I can bring you all up to speed. As many of you know, the company was founded just five years ago with the goal of providing..."

Or . . .

2. "Good morning. I know everyone in this room is concerned about the state of the company, and I called this meeting today to offer you reassurance. We've had some tough quarters, but we expect to be back on solid footing by the fourth quarter of this year. We're a young company, as you know, and we were founded with the goal of providing . . ."

Which option—1 or 2—suits the audience best? Both approaches are set up to convey similar background information to the audience. But one is designed to be far more audience-centric than the other. If you chose 2, you're right. Addressing, right up front, what might be on audience members' minds is clearly the more audience-centric choice. In this case, the company's performance and the need for reassurance (or other news) is akin to having an 800-pound gorilla in the middle of the room; it's a huge "what's in it for me?" and needs to be dealt with ASAP.

Now, which option do you think suits the audience best in this next scenario?

I'm the chief marketing officer of a company and, in narrowing down my selection of a new interactive ad agency, I have invited the finalists to make a presentation. What am I thinking about and what would I most want to hear in these presentations?

1. "Thank you for inviting us to present. We're thrilled to be finalists. We'd like to take the next forty-five minutes to introduce our firm, walk you through some relevant examples of our work on behalf of other clients, and then talk about your project and what we have in mind for you."
Or . . .

2. "Thank you for inviting us. We're thrilled to be here and to share with you what we think will be a killer interactive campaign idea for you. We've gone out on a limb here, and we came up with some ideas for you based on what we know so far. We'd like to share those, get a discussion going, and then we can show you our firm's portfolio of work, if we still have time at the end."

I'm hoping number 2 is the clear winner for you. If I am the potential client, I am practically panting with "what's in it for me?" anticipation. So the second approach suits me perfectly. I'd much rather hear, right up front, what ideas they have for me. I'm probably also curious about their portfolio and what they've accomplished for other clients, but I'm champing at the bit to hear what they've got for me.

There are some arbitrary conventions out there that prevent us from being audience-centric in meetings and presentations. One of those conventions is that in a new business pitch, we should give our background first and then address the client's specific needs or issues. I would reverse that in order to be audience-centric: Audiences, especially clients, first want to hear what's in it for them. We also often assume that in meetings we need to do a lot of stage-setting before we tell the audience what we want them to know or do. Again, I would advocate that you tell them what they need to know right away and then backfill with the stage-setting.

Another arbitrary practice that violates audience-centricity is the standard, one-hour presentation time slot at industry conferences, in which many speakers cleverly offer five to ten key points that they want you to know and take away.

But if I'm attending a conference, is it realistic that I will remember each of the five to ten key points covered by each of the eight speakers on each day of the event? How many key points can I, or will I, retain from each presenter? Maybe one, if I'm lucky. Up to three, if I have a remarkable memory. Or more, if I took great notes or if there's a handout (assuming I even refer to those materials after the conference). Conferences are not typically designed to be audience-centric; rather, with the best of intentions, they are usually geared toward downloading as much material as possible.

Ultimately the question for you as a speaker is this: Which end result do you prefer? Standing in front of a group and being comprehensive, saying everything you know and have to say on a topic? Or being selective and targeted and saying something— even just one thing—that actually resonates with your listeners and sticks in their minds?

Consider the word "present." I have been using it as a verb, but if you look at it as a noun, it's present, as in gift. Think about audience-centricity as a gift to your audiences. As with birthday or holiday gifts, people love something they can use, enjoy, or learn from. You should plan to give a present every time you present! If you want to be that speaker who is memorable, then be extremely selective and targeted. Take a few extra minutes and identify a big idea, a "so what," or a key takeaway for your audience, and then prioritize exactly what and how you're going to present.

Take a cue from Andy Murray and be a selfless speaker; empathize with your (oh, so patient and supportive) audience. Know that they're listening, and anticipate what they're thinking and feeling. Even though Murray was experiencing a crushing personal defeat, he resisted the urge to deliver a personal message and instead offered a message that was meaningful to his audience: a parting, but lasting, gift. Try to avoid Michael Jordan's misstep of using the podium to tell stories that may mean a lot to you but have little value—and, as in his case, may even be offensive—to your audience. Reminiscing about a career is what a Hall of Fame induction speech calls for, but there's still an audience to consider.

Here's the ultimate shortcut play for being audience-centric: Instead of sitting down and thinking, *Okay, what do I want to say to the group tomorrow?* sit down and think, *Okay, what does the group need to know or hear tomorrow?* Start with them, not you. Shift your thoughts away from your own interest in your topic for a minute and put your head straight into the needs, interests, and concerns of your audience as the first step in your preparation. That just might be all you need to do to avoid the missteps of obsessing about your nerves rather than your audience, running over the time limit, reading your slides, or not preparing ahead. If you know what you want to give them, you are ready!

Time and attention are scarce and precious for everyone, businesspeople and sports fans alike. The absolute key to being an effective speaker is to think about—*really think about*—and respect your audiences.

Playing to Your Fans

1.   **Think.** Think about what's interesting and important to your audience—not just to you—before and during your talk.

2.   **Prioritize!** You no doubt have volumes you can or want to say on any given occasion, but you need to prioritize according to who your audience is, what they care about, and how much time you have. Your audience's time and attention are precious.

3.   **Identify your "play of the day"—or your present.** What do you have to share or give to your audience that will satisfy their "what's in it for me?" and create a memorable experience for them?

Self-Assessment Exercises

Think about the last time you attended a conference or sat through someone else's presentation. What was your reaction? Can you remember a useful takeaway (or two or three)? If not, what would you have liked to hear from the speaker? Jot down any thoughts—positive or negative—about that presentation here.

_____
_____
_____
_____
_____
_____
_____
_____
_____
_____
_____
_____
_____
_____
_____
_____
_____
_____
_____

Now think about the last speech or presentation you gave. Who was your audience? Did you carefully consider their interests? Prioritize your material? Come up with a useful and meaningful takeaway? Take a second to identify the self-interest or bias your audience had. Did you address it? How?

_____

_____

_____

_____

_____

_____

_____

_____

_____

_____

_____

How would you reorganize or rearrange your talk or presentation now? Write down some options or ideas here.

_____

_____

_____

_____

_____

_____

_____

_____

_____

CHAPTER 3

SQUARING TO BUNT

"Transparency shows."

In 2003, during the investigation into steroid use among Major League Baseball players, many players issue denials. Yankees first baseman Jason Giambi never denies his use to the grand jury, but it takes him four more years to publicly acknowledge it and apologize.

"I was wrong for doing that stuff," Giambi admits to *USA Today* in 2007. "What we should have done a long time ago was stand up—players, ownership, everybody—and said: 'We made a mistake.'"[6]

Not only apologizing, but also admitting he should have done so earlier, wins Giambi kudos in the media as well as public goodwill. While his comments make Major League Baseball and Yankees management squirm a bit, *The Nation*'s sports correspondent, Dave Zirin, notes, "[Giambi's] statement last week constitutes the most honest and interesting talk in two years . . ."[7] The ballplayer's transparency helps him to move on from the investigation and continue his career.

In contrast, we have the example of Tiger Woods and his very scripted, über-controlled February 2010 press conference, following his very public November 2009 domestic incident and its fallout. He is so overly coached—probably by lawyers more than by PR people—that he offers just about everything except a sincere explanation for why he is finally speaking publicly and what he hopes to accomplish by holding the press conference. Woods begins the press conference by saying, "I know people want to find out how I could be so selfish and so foolish. People want to know how I could have done these things to my wife Elin and to my children."[8] However, he never answers those very questions.

He is open about some of the facts of the incident, and he's very apologetic, but he's not transparent about what led to the incident and what his objective is for the press conference. It's a show of shows, for sure, but it gives too little to his very curious audience.

The bottom line with transparency is this: If something is true and real and you're thinking it, feeling it, or wanting it, then communicate it. When a batter squares to bunt, people know what's coming. You might as well be the leader who also lets people know what's coming. Be straight up with information as well as with your feelings and reactions. When faced with a crisis or criticism, call it out, tell it like it is, and own up, rather than being the Grand Master of Duck and Cover, Chief Whitewasher, or Captain Backtrack. The discerning audiences you face will give you props for being up front, direct, and genuine.

"Transparency" has become one of those twenty-first century buzzwords, used to measure how open, honest, and aboveboard corporate or government officials are. It's an important word, and it has found its way into our common vocabulary with good reason: We want and need more transparency. Audiences demand it.

Barely a generation or two ago, the public took things on nearly blind faith. If an authority figure said something, then it was true. That model started to unravel beginning with Watergate in the early 1970s, when the American public was introduced to a grand political cover-up. A new public scrutiny emerged in the post-Watergate era, and with that, people became harsher judges of their leaders.

In fact, a Gallup poll measuring historical trends in trust in government from 1972 to 2013 shows that in 1972, 73 percent of respondents had a "fair amount" or "great deal" of trust in the executive branch (the office of the president of the United States) versus 51 percent in 2013, forty-one years later. The same survey for the legislative branch (US Congress) shows that in 1972, 71 percent of respondents had a fair amount or great deal of trust in Congress, versus 34 percent in 2013. I think what's particularly interesting here is the consistency of the trust numbers in 1972; 73 percent and 71 percent might indicate that there was wide-spread trust in government without making a distinction between branches. By contrast, the numbers in 2013 show much more discernment, with an almost 20-point gap in how much people trust those two branches of government.[9]

In its annual "exploration of trust," global PR firm Edelman takes a closer look at trust and the relationship between trust in business and in government around the world through its Edelman Trust Barometer. While tens of thousands of respondents trusted the institutions of business more than government—by more than 20 percentage points in the US—their trust in the leaders of business and government is low. According to Edelman's 2014 report, "CEOs and government leaders remain at the bottom of the list for both Informed and General Publics, with extremely low trust levels on key metrics. Only one in four General Public respondents trusts business leaders to correct issues, and even fewer—one in five—to tell the truth and make ethical and moral decisions."[10]

Over the last forty years, we have become a society that values harsh truths and authenticity over comforting appearances. The opportunities created by the Internet and digital media have given us windows onto people and organizations that we didn't have before. These windows make it easier to access and scrutinize all kinds of information. People can now find, opine about, or even fabricate "truths" online. More important, average people—your customers, employees, and peers—are always on the lookout for truth and authenticity, and, whether consciously or not, they're running your words and your conduct through those filters.

Our perception of all public figures, including professional athletes, is almost an exaggerated version of this phenomenon of access and scrutiny. We decide, without knowing these people and without ever having been in their presence, whether they're genuinely admirable and worship-worthy or just full of themselves—and full of crap. Transparency can make or break our opinion of them.

There are two kinds of transparency: One deals with being open, honest, and forthright with *information*; the other, being open, honest, and forthright with *feelings or reactions*. Transparency calls for truth and authenticity in both cases.

When you speak publicly, transparency applies to both your content and your delivery. Are you transparent in words and emotion? Do they match? What does your demeanor suggest about how authentic and trustworthy you are? Are you trying to spin the situation, are you holding back, or are you spilling it all out? And are you acknowledging your feelings? For example, would you say something like, "This situation is emotional for me, so bear with me while I get it all out" or "I wish I could say more, but I can't at this time" or "I have tough news to share, but I'm going to try and put the best possible light on it so you see the bright side"?

Truth and Authenticity: The Facts

In Jason Giambi's case, he openly admitted wrongdoing and expressed sincere regret. While he had and will always have some detractors, Giambi's image has seemed to weather the baseball steroid controversy better than others'. It's interesting to compare what happened to Giambi in 2007 and to Alex Rodriguez in 2014.

At the time of Giambi's admission, ESPN.com and other news outlets noted that Major League Baseball Commissioner Bud Selig was not disciplining Giambi, explicitly because the ballplayer had cooperated with investigators and was also doing valued charitable work.[11] Some years later and in connection with the very same issue of steroid usage, Commissioner Selig levied the most severe disciplinary action against Alex Rodriguez—he was banned from an entire season—precisely because he had gone to great lengths to dodge the drug issue, despite a tidal wave of evidence suggesting that Rodriguez had used banned substances during the period in question. An unnamed baseball source was quoted in the *New York Daily News* as saying that A-Rod "would have been better off admitting he got drugs . . . and tried to make a case for 50 games [suspension] as a first-time violator."[12]

In Tiger Woods's case, the golfer admitted wrongdoing and expressed regret, but did so in such a scripted and controlled way that, as Romesh Ratnesar and Bill Saporito—two *Time* magazine editors who were longtime followers of Woods's career—noted, he was "wooden" and that "showing humility . . . will be absolutely essential" if he hoped to win back the public.[13] Timothy Coombs, PhD, a professor of crisis communication at Eastern Illinois University, called the Woods apology "an epic fail," noting that Tiger's apology was neither clear nor compelling.[14]

Managing a fall from grace—for an athlete or any other public figure—requires opening oneself up with as much honest information and genuine feeling as possible. What's at stake are the obvious desirables of likeability, credibility, trust, and respect.

As we've seen in the examples of Giambi and Woods, the demand for transparency spikes during difficult times, such as a crisis or when responding to criticism. Transparency, however, is not just for fallen—or falling—heroes. When employed as part of a leader's voice, tone, and attitude, transparency can provide a valuable ounce of prevention for a cure that all too often far exceeds the proverbial pound. It often takes a full ton to recapture the ground lost, in terms of reputation and credibility, if that's even possible. Hence the case for being a leader who is open, honest, and forthright on a regular basis.

Taking a look at leadership in the twenty-first century, Harvard Business School held a Centennial Summit in 2008 and reported, "The basics of leadership haven't changed much over the last 100 years. Leadership is about acting with integrity, persuading others to follow (because they want to, not because they have to), creating a culture of openness, having discipline, communicating clearly, and forging relationships built on mutual confidence. Not much changes during a crisis."[15] Basic, and still compelling.

Truth and Authenticity: The Feelings

Transparency for business leaders is also about being real and accessible human beings: sharing not just the business strategy but also the thinking and motivations behind it; sharing not just the quarterly or annual numbers but also the sense of pride or disappointment that goes with them; sharing not just the news of a big piece of new business but also the hopes and fears that accompany it. It's the facts, the feelings, and the context.

Transparency in communication keeps the audience's intuition filter clear, which means that what you say and how you say it has a better chance of flowing straight through to your audience the way you intended. Transparency is owning the good and the bad, saying what you mean and meaning what you say. It's answering your critics not with defensiveness and counterattacks but with direct, open, honest truths and realities. It's about being as open a book as you can be without jeopardizing your business or other people.

Some executives even pledge transparency. Take the case of Mary Barra, CEO of General Motors. In April 2014, she was barely a few months into the top job with the auto giant when she was called to testify before Congress about why it took the company ten years to recall cars with faulty ignition switches. According to her prepared remarks, Barra said, "Sitting here today, I cannot tell you why it took years for a safety defect to be announced . . . but I can tell you that we will find out. When we have answers, we will be fully transparent with you, with our regulators, and with our customers."[16] "Fully transparent" has become a requirement and an expectation.

But what about criticism? How does transparency apply to that?

I've observed over the years that criticism can be a quite perplexing and potentially contentious phenomenon, especially for those on the receiving end. Unless it's deliberately malicious, criticism is usually true or has some element of truth. Even better, if it's true, there's usually a good rationale for it.

Yet the natural reaction to being criticized—especially publicly criticized—is to block, tackle, and defend. Instead, my preferred strategy, and the one I use when I counsel clients, is to pause and think for a moment, stay calm, and then stand tall and own the criticism if it's true and if there's good reasoning behind it.

In other words, I tend to look at criticism as bad packaging for good material. Here are two examples.

In his first bid to become mayor, a client of mine faced what turned out to be rather ironic criticism from his opponent. The criticism was focused, in fact, on my guy's strongest attribute.

My client, an attorney and urban planner by training, had been a state legislator and owned a consulting business that specialized in community planning, environmental assessment, and public land use. His opponent had also held public office and many positions in public-sector bureaucracies. As the race got closer to the general election, the main criticism leveled against my candidate by his opponent was that he was a "dreamer, not a doer." The implication was that because my client was a planner, he would spend his days staring at the sky, thinking about the future, and not taking necessary action on the day-to-day business of the city. I recall a day in the campaign office when it felt like the opposition winds were blowing strongly against us. A group of advisers had assembled around the conference room table to discuss how to respond to the "dreamer" attacks. The discussion produced ideas for counterattacks and creative ways to portray my client as action-oriented. And that's when I had my *aha!* moment and thought to myself: *Hold on a minute! He is a dreamer-planner, and that's a good thing. After all, what forward-looking, fast-growing metropolitan area wouldn't want an urban planner for mayor?* The message and tone of campaign communications stayed its unapologetic course, and my client won the election.

The second anecdote comes from the corporate side of my coaching practice. Over the years I have worked with executives in some rather unpopular businesses such as surface and underground mining, medical waste incineration, oil refining, and other "industrial polluters." These executives are often under fire 24/7 from community groups, neighbors, local governments, the media, and average citizens. Yet their companies often perform necessary tasks—unpleasant perhaps, but necessary.

One particular company, which operated a medical waste incinerator, was being torn to shreds in the local news media for being a major contributor to area pollution. There were cries for public officials to kick the company out—of the state, that is. Public outrage had grown to a point where it was disproportionate to the actual harm done.

In preparation for editorial board meetings at local newspapers, I worked with company executives so they would be able to calmly acknowledge the criticism yet balance it with an open, straightforward explanation of what they burn and why. For one, they were located near a major cancer hospital, and the residue from chemotherapy had to be incinerated; otherwise, if thrown in the landfill with ordinary garbage, the chemotherapy toxins would leach into the groundwater and create an entirely different public health issue. In other words, there was good reason for the incineration they were being criticized for; it was the preferred alternative in this case, and so defensiveness or combativeness were just not necessary.

The executives had their editorial board meetings and were matter-of-factly open and straightforward about what they do, how, and why. They owned it. In the end, the newspapers began to understand the business better, which led to a more balanced perspective in their reporting from that point forward.

Of course, some critics will never go away, as football great Mike Ditka so perfectly illustrated when he said, "What's the difference between a three-week-old puppy and a sportswriter? In six weeks, the puppy stops whining." Nonetheless, by being transparent, you have a shot at disarming the cynics and commentators when you're under fire. And under normal or calm conditions, being transparent in your communications can capture the attention and win the affection of your audiences. Or, no less desirable, it can neutralize strong opposition or criticism.

Similarly, when faced with the usual ups and downs of business, you want to be that leader who shares personal excitement, disappointment, frustration—or any of the various emotions that professional successes and failures can bring—in a way that is authentic, believable, and real. Emotion makes a profound, lasting impression on an audience; it can motivate, inspire, and ultimately connect and engage. When it comes to what audiences retain after a talk, impressions trump information every time. As the famed poet and writer Maya Angelou once said, "I've learned that people will forget what you said, people will forget what you did, but people will never forget how you made them feel."

There are, understandably, barriers to being perfectly transparent. One barrier related to information is the need to maintain confidentiality or to use discretion, which is justified in many situations. Another barrier pertains to emotional transparency. Some people may resist it because the more traditional definition of leadership embraces stoicism over "opening up" or being vulnerable in any way.

Neither of these barriers is bad per se, and full openness and disclosure is not called for in every instance, but a willingness to be open, honest, and forthright with your audiences under the right conditions can be a winning proposition for a leader. Being open, candid, and real in your communications is ultimately a very appealing and connecting style.

Practically speaking, here are some ways to employ transparency in your day-to-day business communications—for example, in a meeting, presentation, or speech.

In your opening. For any of these communications opportunities, you have a win, a desired outcome, or a hopeful takeaway in mind, right? There is something you would like your audience—even an audience of one—to think, or know, or do, or feel after you are finished talking. If so, then spoon-feed it, spell it out, tell them right up front. Otherwise, left to their own devices, members of an audience are unlikely to connect the dots—and if they do, they still may not end up where you want them to be. You have to spoon-feed whatever it is you want your audience to think, know, do, or feel. Be that direct with them. Put your intentions and your desired outcome right out there. Open with it. Get your audience to focus where you want them to focus. No guessing at how the dots connect.

In the middle. A simple call-out—for example, of a point with special significance or a certain feeling you get when you address an issue—is transparency at its best. Not only is it a matter of the speaker being real, it is also a helpful trail marker for the audience. For instance, letting an audience know that this next point you're going to cover is one that gets you excited or frustrated, or one that you have given a lot of thought to, helps guide the audience toward a better understanding of context—that is, where you're coming from—and the relative importance or significance of the points you're making.

At the end. Preparing a talk is not like writing an essay. For your audience, listening to a speaker is a different experience than reading a document. Listeners will grasp what you give them, both in impression and information, but perhaps more in impression, as Maya Angelou and others have pointed out. Consider, then, how you might leave your audience with a positive impression or a good feeling. Wrap up with something personal about the experience of being in the room with them, by telling them how you have viewed them as an audience, or by sharing how you have felt about addressing them on your topic. And then tell them again what it is that you hope they will think, know, do, or feel when they leave the room. Conclude by making the whole experience transparent—and therefore memorable.

Squaring to Bunt

1. **Transparency comes in two forms—informational and emotional.** Think about ways you can be more transparent. One easy way is to let people know what play (like a bunt) they can expect; try spelling out your desired outcome in the opening seconds of your meetings and presentations.

2. **Pay attention to crises and critics.** You don't necessarily need to run or fight. Be open to owning your truths and realities, both bad and good. It scores big reputational points for credibility and trust.

3. **Audiences are smart.** Scrutiny and skepticism can be harsh. Leaders, like public figures, are subject to both. Be as open, honest, and forthright as you can. Be real.

Practice Exercises

Think about the lowest or weakest point in your business or professional life. What was it?

_____

_____

_____

_____

_____

_____

_____

_____

_____

_____

What aspect of it makes you feel vulnerable or uncomfortable to talk about?

_____

_____

_____

_____

_____

_____

_____

_____

Can you come up with a way to discuss or address it in an open and direct way?

_____

_____

_____

_____

_____

_____

_____

_____

_____

_____

_____

_____

_____

_____

_____

_____

_____

_____

_____

_____

_____

_____

_____

_____

_____

Have you ever had to answer questions about a business problem or crisis? What happened?

_____

_____

_____

_____

_____

_____

_____

_____

_____

_____

_____

Write down the questions you remember and practice answering them with transparency in both information and emotion. Make notes about your answers if that would be helpful.

_____

_____

_____

_____

_____

_____

_____

_____

_____

CHAPTER 4

ALLEY-OOP

"Graciousness scores points."

Lou Gehrig's 1939 speech announcing his retirement comes shortly after his diagnosis with amyotrophic lateral sclerosis (ALS), the disease that will take his life just two years in the future. Fans already know of his struggles with his health. This is how Gehrig chooses to tell the world he will be unable to continue to play baseball:

> "Fans, for the past two weeks you have been reading about the bad break I got. Yet today I consider myself the luckiest man on the face of the earth. I have been in ballparks for seventeen years and have never received anything but kindness and encouragement from you fans . . . Sure, I'm lucky . . . I close in saying that I might have been given a bad break, but I've got an awful lot to live for. Thank you."

Gehrig's farewell speech to his fans is a textbook example of graciousness setting the tone to help the audience deal with sadness or loss.

In contrast, Dan Gilbert, majority owner of the Cleveland Cavaliers basketball team, shows no such graciousness when faced with his own trouble: losing hometown hero LeBron James to the Miami Heat. In his 2010 open letter to Cleveland fans, Gilbert demonstrates vindictiveness, bitterness, and poor sportsmanship as he publicly bemoans James's decision:

> "I can tell you that this shameful display of selfishness and betrayal by one of our very own has shifted our 'motivation' to previously unknown and previously never experienced levels . . . This shocking act of disloyalty from our homegrown 'chosen one' sends the exact opposite lesson of what we would want our children to learn. And 'who' we would want them to grow up to become . . .
>
> "The self-declared former 'King' will be taking the 'curse' with him down south. And until he does 'right' by Cleveland and Ohio, James (and the town where he plays) will unfortunately own this dreaded spell and bad karma."

In response, then-NBA Commissioner David Stern fined Gilbert $100,000 for the letter's contents. And sports columnist William Rhoden of the *New York Times* stood by James, stating that Gilbert's "venomous, face-saving personal attack," and the "wrath of jersey-burning fans," vindicated James's decision to quit the Cavaliers.[17]

I'm not sure Dan Gilbert fully understood the concept of karma when he issued his threatening prediction. One can certainly understand his feelings of disappointment, even anger, but the sports world is full of examples and opportunities where men and women have had to rise above those feelings and be gracious. As tennis player Jim Courier once said, "Sportsmanship for me is when a guy walks off the court and you really can't tell whether he won or lost, when he carries himself with pride either way." Exactly. Graciousness.

Graciousness is not about being humble; it's about being generous, even—especially!—under duress. It's about being your highest, best self and making the unselfish, alley-oop pass to the other guy, whoever that may be: teammate, opponent, owner, or fan. It's about helping your audience through difficult situations in the best way possible. Graciousness is just as important when things are going well as when they're not. It's about sharing the glory of scoring. It's about showing leadership through generous attitudes and actions.

Executives are often called upon to speak publicly and tell their company story, especially when it's a success story. There are two ways to handle this, and you probably have seen both in action: one is to tell the story, hitting all the highlights and taking credit for the successes, and the other is to tell the story, touching on the highs and lows and talking about how the team came together, how friends and colleagues pitched in, and how clients and suppliers have been phenomenal partners in the growth. Which approach do you find more appealing? Probably the latter, because the speaker's graciousness in telling the success story is inherently more appealing.

In Diana Nyad's Ted Talk at TedWomen 2013, which she delivers just three months after her historic swim from Cuba to Florida, she captivates the audience with tales of the ups and downs, thoughts and feelings, and challenges and breakthroughs during her fifth attempt at this notoriously difficult swim. In describing her mindset upon reaching the beach in Key West, having finally and successfully completed the feat, she offers this alley-oop, with her voice and gestures cementing the impression it leaves: "All those orations that I had practiced just to get myself through some training swims as motivation—it wasn't like that. It was a very real moment, with that crowd, with my team. We did it. I didn't do it. *We* did it. And we'll never forget it. It'll always be part of us."[18]

We would have understood if, at sixty-four, with four unsuccessful attempts behind her, thirty-five years of trying, and fifty-three hours of grueling ocean time, Diana took sole credit for her achievement. But she shared it.

When communicating around challenges, loss, difficulties, or outright defeat, hitting notes of graciousness is hard. There may be hurt, anger, or deep disappointment involved, all of which can cloud a person's ability to be his or her best self. Or there may be intense competition in the air, which also makes clearheaded, articulate graciousness more difficult to draw on. Finding it somehow, even under these circumstances, is what distinguishes you as a leader.

Other than publicly venting his profound anger and disappointment, Dan Gilbert accomplished nothing for his franchise or for his city. To many, he looked and sounded like a sore loser. That was his choice; another option would have been to find the words to thank "King James" for his contributions, wish him well, and then focus on rallying the team and the city. Gilbert was in a position to lead and show Cleveland fans the way forward, albeit minus the team's superstar. But he ranted instead. (As a note, Gilbert said very little when four years later James announced his return to Cleveland.) There are some, I'm sure, who think

Gilbert's display of rage demonstrated leadership in the face of adversity. According to that view, perhaps he led, but he did so using anger and hostility. That's a style choice. Is that the style you would choose for yourself and your organization?

Yes, it may be difficult to get to higher ground, but speakers sound more appealing when they're communicating positive and hopeful messages rather than negative and angry ones. They're more likely to get things done, too, in that carrot-versus-stick way.

In a study of the qualities and impact of positive and negative words published by EPJ Data Science in 2012, it was noted "that the process of communication between humans, which is known to optimize information transfer, also creates a bias towards positive emotional content . . . The expression of positive emotions increases the level of communication and strengthens social links." The study found that the frequency of usage for positive words is higher than for negative words, but that negative words carry more information, because they serve a different purpose, namely, "that of transmitting highly informative and relevant events," such as a threat or danger.[19] Positive words, on the other hand, lead to more cooperation.

If we step back, then, and look at the types of communications leaders are most often engaged in—motivating, inspiring, selling, persuading, influencing—we find an imperative for more positive words and phrasing. Leaders are responsible for cultivating teams and for maintaining and building their franchise, the brand, and the business. As former Chrysler CEO Lee Iacocca once said, "Management is nothing more than motivating people."

Just like an alley-oop pass to a teammate, "lobbing one to the other guy" can also score points. Being gracious in your communications is often unexpected in certain circumstances and can therefore be unnerving to the competition or opposition.

In my work with political candidates, I've seen that "making love and peace, not hate and war" works best when it comes to rhetoric. Audiences—in this case, voters—can be put off by the negativity and confrontations that candidates often engage in during debates or media interviews. It can be a turnoff. On the other hand, they seem willing to listen and offer support if the candidate sounds more positive.

Let me share a bit of advice I always give candidates. There are some basic questions they need to be prepared to answer, including, "How are you different from your opponent?" My advice is to first address the similarities—that is, to list a few admirable traits they both have in common—and then get to the parts where they differ. So, the answer might go something like this: "Candidate X and I are both extremely family-oriented and dedicated public servants who want the best for all residents in terms of jobs and education for our children, but we see some of the issues a little differently . . ." A little alley-oop—and then the slam dunk!

Here you can see the rule of first impressions at play. If you come out swinging and then soften up, people are likely to remember the swinging. If you come out gently and graciously and *then* take subtle swings, the graciousness is likely to stick. Positives first.

As we saw with Gilbert's rant, the same is true for athletes. We might have been entertained by the team owner's remarks, but we probably won't remember what he said, only that he first lost his superstar and then his temper. The gladiator can be quite entertaining for a moment, but the gentleman will endure. This is probably why Lou Gehrig's farewell speech has been remembered for seventy-plus years.

In the face of difficulty, there is always room for a leader to step in and frame public discourse or sentiment. This is similar to what clergy do when they deliver a eulogy, offering the comfort and perspective their audience needs in that moment of loss. You, as a leader in an organization, will no doubt face moments when your audience is counting on you to tell them what they should do with their mixed, confusing, or sad feelings. And if the moment is big enough, what you say should be something that will help them move forward and that will endure.

Johnson & Johnson CEO James E. Burke was widely praised for handling one of the worst corporate crises in one of the best and most proactive ways during the Tylenol poisoning episode in 1982. Seven people, including one child, died from cyanide-laced Tylenol pills in the Chicago area. From a crisis management point of view, Burke's actions and words were exemplary. In response to the 1982 events, he ordered one of the first massive product recalls, pulling 31 million bottles (with a retail value of $100 million) of the nation's best-selling pain reliever from shelves across the country and replacing them as soon as possible with what was at the time a brilliant innovation: tamper-resistant packaging, a quick-turnaround company initiative that Burke personally oversaw. The entire effort saved the Tylenol brand and reinforced J&J's reputation and its long-term shareholder confidence.

From a communication standpoint, Burke was lauded for making himself available and accessible to the media during the crisis and for offering comments that were marked by compassion, genuine concern for the public's safety, and open acknowledgment of the importance of the public's trust. "People forget how we built up such a big and important franchise," said Burke. "It was based on trust."[20]

In subsequent decades, Burke was showered with accolades for saving and rebuilding a brand and the corporation behind it and for his candor in the face of a crisis that threatened to take down both. In 2000 he was awarded the Presidential Medal of Freedom by President Bill Clinton, and three years later Burke was recognized by *Fortune* magazine as one of history's ten greatest CEOs. Yet despite all of the attention and acclaim accorded him, in 2003 Burke reflected on the crisis: "When crises occurred that we never could have foreseen, our customers stuck by us in ways we never could have imagined. A company credo that put customers first and shareholders last ultimately benefited both groups."[21]

Burke's comments contained subtle deflections of praise along with a sincere sharing of recognition with others. Graciousness and leadership. Period.

In stark contrast, let's look at the public remarks of former BP CEO Tony Hayward following the Deepwater Horizon disaster in 2010. When the explosion and sinking of an oil rig caused dangerous and unprecedented amounts of oil to spill into the Gulf of Mexico, the company took many of the right communications measures, including apologizing and reassuring the public through ads and public statements. But then came the CEO's career-defining gaffe: In the face of loss of lives and livelihoods, Hayward said, on camera, "There's no one who wants this thing over more than I do, I'd like my life back."[22] His lack of self-awareness and sensitivity concerning his audience met such broad criticism that Hayward resigned and was replaced a few short months after the incident.

So how do you cast your communications in the language and tone of graciousness? I suggest that for every situation, even the most difficult, you can find points of positivity, optimism, or gratitude. They're in there; you just have to dig deep and find them. In moments of greatness and success, that can be as simple as spreading the wealth—offering credit or congratulations to others, sharing the spotlight, handing off a pass to someone else to let that person score. In more difficult moments, it's not as easy or obvious. In those moments, your questions to yourself as a gracious communicator must be:

What's right?

What's good here?

What am I hopeful about?

What makes us successful or special, and what motivates us?

What do we have to look forward to tomorrow?

John Gerzema's book *The Athena Doctrine* argues that traits like gratitude—sometimes disparaged as too "feminine"—are actually crucial to effective leadership. *Inc.*'s Leigh Buchanan praised Gerzema's observations, saying, "We have progressed from command-and-control (roughly through the 1980s) to empower-and-track (the 1990s to mid-2000s) to connect-and-nurture (today). Increasingly, the chief executive role is taking its place among the caring professions. It takes a tender person to lead a tough company."[23]

Trying Out Graciousness

Use this exercise to practice habits of graciousness as a leader:

You are the CEO of a company that develops switching software for telecom companies. Heather, your senior vice president of sales, has left to join a competitor, taking with her one of your oldest and largest client accounts. You need to address the entire sales team to keep them focused and motivated for the near term, or at least until you sort through the organizational upheaval caused by her departure. Naturally, feelings of bewilderment, betrayal, loss, and fear are present for you and for the sales crew, but you have to rise above those and motivate the troops. Below are some perfectly reasonable options for your remarks to the team. Read them and then pick the one you think displays the most gracious (not to mention audience-centric and transparent) approach.

1. "Heather's departure leaves a huge hole for all of us, and we are sorry to see her go. We wish her luck in her next endeavor. We're unsure at this point exactly who will take her place and how we will plug up certain holes she leaves, but be assured, we will do both. You all are very important to this organization, and please know that your efforts and patience during this transition are appreciated. I will update you as I know more. In the meantime, though, please carry on with your strong work. Our sales force is one of the greatest assets we have in this organization, so thank you and carry on. We will be just fine."
Or . . .

2. "One of the most challenging times for any team is when there's change. Change presents us with a true test of our depth and strength. I believe we have that depth and strength and that this particular change will open new opportunities that maybe we wouldn't have imagined without it. There's no doubt we will miss Heather. We thank her for her many contributions over the years and wish her all the best. But now it's time to rise to the challenge this transition presents us with. It's time to hit the

'refresh' button and see what pops up on our screens. I have no doubt that this ultimately will be good for all of us. I welcome the challenge, and I am excited to see what happens next. In the meantime, let's pull together, share ideas, and continue to be the best sales team in the industry."

They're both good, right? Perfectly polite, straightforward, and appropriate. But which one takes it to the next level? To a level of graciousness befitting a leader?

Number 1 empathizes, it's audience-centric and transparent, and there's certainly nothing about it that would suggest it's not gracious. Yet it lacks a certain higher-level viewpoint and positivity. It's a bit too tactical in nature—though that is understandable—and it doesn't do a lot to raise spirits and keep the team motivated. It almost sounds like a perfunctory or obligatory "we lost an important person" message.

Number 2 goes straight up to 30,000 feet and provides a higher-level viewpoint, right off the bat. It's about change, and it goes so far as to lay the groundwork for change being exciting, not just something to be endured or survived. This option builds in some anticipation and suggests there will be room for the team to give input. It says there may be new opportunities ahead. It is audience-centric and transparent but also gracious in its hopefulness and positivity.

When keeping a group of people motivated or achieving a turnaround in attitudes during challenging times is called for, it can feel a lot like pulling a heavy sled through snow. But optimism and gratitude—laced with a bit of confidence—can help you pull the heaviest load through the biggest blizzard. Use your most positive strengths, your optimism, and your gratitude, along with your genuine caring and passion, to help you. This is, above all else, what distinguishes a leader from everyone else.

Finding and getting comfortable with your gracious voice takes a certain internal calmness and confidence, as does passing the ball and letting someone else score. You have to have faith in the play, know that it works, and use it in good times and bad. Positivity, caring, and nurturing should all be on your checklist; if you cover one or more of those, you have very likely hit your graciousness notes.

Alley-oop

1. **Stay positive.** Everyone sounds better—more motivating and more appealing—when they use positive rather than negative words.

2. **Be gracious.** Being gracious not only reflects well on you and your leadership style, but because it is often unexpected, it can be unnerving to the competition or opposition.

3. **Take an optimistic stance.** Try looking at even a difficult situation through the lenses of positivity, optimism, and gratitude. You'll be surprised at what you can come up with.

Self-Assessment Exercises

Think back to a recent personal or business success. What happened?

_____

_____

_____

_____

_____

_____

_____

_____

_____

How did you characterize it to others, publicly or in private?

_____

_____

_____

_____

_____

_____

_____

_____

_____

_____

Did you share—or could you have shared—the credit for the victory with others? How?

_____

_____

_____

_____

_____

_____

_____

_____

_____

Did you use it—or could you have used it—to motivate others? How?

_____

_____

_____

_____

_____

_____

_____

_____

_____

_____

_____

_____

_____

Did anyone else offer praise for this or a similar situation? In what ways were they gracious in describing their own or others' contributions?

_____

_____

_____

_____

_____

_____

_____

_____

_____

Now consider a recent—or not so recent—difficult time. What happened?

_____

_____

_____

_____

_____

_____

_____

_____

_____

_____

_____

Did you have to step in and lead others through trying circumstances? What did you say?

_____

_____

_____

_____

_____

_____

_____

_____

_____

Looking back, could you have done anything differently? How?

_____

_____

_____

_____

_____

_____

_____

_____

_____

_____

_____

_____

How would you handle the same situation today? Would you be able to turn it into a teaching or motivating moment? Can you outline what your talking points might be?

_____

_____

_____

_____

_____

_____

_____

_____

_____

_____

_____

_____

_____

_____

_____

_____

_____

_____

_____

_____

_____

_____

_____

CHAPTER 5

PUNT PLAY

"Brevity makes great bling."

In 2008 the Boston Celtics win the NBA championship. In an interview after the final game, coach Doc Rivers is asked what he told the team at their first meeting at training camp months earlier. His response: "Defense. We play defense and we are going to win a world championship, and that's exactly what they did." He says it all in just one brief comment.

LeBron James's move to the Miami Heat gives us a contrasting example: how to draw something out to the point of frustration. James announces in 2010 that he is leaving his hometown team in an hour-long ESPN special ("The Decision"), with the actual announcement coming more than halfway through a program that has already been hyped for weeks.

Even though the TV special has raised money for charity, immediate public reaction is negative: James had simply taken too much time and assumed too much interest on the part of the audience. In short, he tried their patience. Sports fans ranted, and sports reporters snickered, but the coup de grâce may have been Steve Carell and Paul Rudd's spoof of "The Decision" during the 2010 ESPYs (Excellence in Sports Performance Yearly Awards).

At that ESPN event, Carell painfully prolongs a mock interview with Rudd by answering question after question in a coyly evasive—and unmistakably tedious—manner.

James, too, seems to have had second thoughts about how that announcement was handled. When he decided to leave the Miami Heat and return to Cleveland for the 2014–15 season, he announced his move in three words that he posted on Instagram and that formed the headline for a concise essay he contributed to *Sports Illustrated*: "I'm Coming Home." In fact, without mentioning "The Decision" in the essay, he leaves readers to wonder if comments like "I'm not having a press conference or a party. After this, it's time to get to work"[24] are a reflective reference to four years earlier. Regardless, his 2014 essay is brief, to the point, and—I would have to add—impressively audience-centric, transparent, and gracious. Four years and two championships later, James could be the shining example of this chapter, and he is poised for true leadership.

Almost predictably, public reaction was overwhelmingly favorable. Almost everyone focused on how exciting the news was for Cleveland, but in a *USA Today Sports* article that day, reporter Laken Litman wrote, "He tastefully announced his decision in an essay in *Sports Illustrated* that he is going home to play for the Cavaliers."[25] Tastefully announced, indeed. Brevity is a winner every time.

When was the last time you or someone you know complained because a speaker was brief? Quite the opposite, right? Like bling, brevity immediately gets our attention. It's a quick way to be memorable and ensure that your audience retains your points. There's nothing quite like brevity for making a lasting impression.

And, just like a successful punt, getting the job done quickly can advance your game strategy and score points.

Regardless of how brilliant or compelling a speaker's material is, audiences get downright annoyed when speakers are long-winded or go over their allotted time. In these cases, even if the content is stellar, the takeaway is a less-than-stellar impression. When people use the words "brief and to the point" to describe a speaker or presenter's performance, it is usually high praise.

In fact, in my coaching practice, executives often come to me for help in "becoming more concise" or "making a point succinctly." Those are common goals for coaching engagements, and it's because the inability to be more concise or to make a point succinctly can be a career blocker.

The opposite is also true; brevity can enhance a career. I worked with a client who was the president of a division of a large publicly traded company. He was about to assume a leadership role with a prominent national industry group, and he and the other four division presidents routinely made formal presentations at the company's quarterly board meetings and at the annual shareholder meeting. He hired me because he believed he lacked the polish, sophistication, and educational background of the other executives; in his words, he wanted to "sound better."

When I met with him for the first time, I was struck by a smart, authentic—yes, quite folksy—and charismatic guy. He was hoping to lose his "twang" and acquire some "fancy" new vocabulary words, but I knew immediately that I wanted to preserve his natural speaking style. My goal was to work with him on being brief—crisp, impactful, and to the point. And that's exactly what we did; we worked on brevity.

At board meetings, he became the guy with one slide, three key points, and very few details to share. He summarized and captured the "so what?" of his division's performance, which was, of course, outlined in much greater detail in the board's briefing book. It became customary for him to speak for only three to five minutes. Despite the high praise he began receiving from the CEO, board members, and even his colleagues, the other division heads continued to deliver long, detailed, multislide narratives of their divisions' performances. My client's reputation—and self-confidence—shot up after just the second quarterly board presentation. He went on to employ the principle of brevity internally with direct reports and externally at his industry group board meetings.

In another example, I watched with genuine (and delighted) surprise as a different client's display of brevity also captured the limelight. I was working with a recently elected official to craft his first inaugural address. His predecessor's speeches were known to exceed an hour. We deliberately kept this one visionary, inspirational . . . and six minutes long. I know it was exactly six minutes only because a reporter timed it and wrote a story that appeared in the next morning's paper, highlighting the address less for its content and more for its refreshing brevity. The words "dynamic" and "signaling change" were in the headline, and the first paragraph of the story said, "Six minutes into his inaugural speech, the beginning of a new era was evident: He stopped talking." Bling, indeed.

Think about the Gettysburg Address. President Lincoln's three-minute speech has resonated for more than 150 years, but no one remembers Edward Everett, who was supposed to be the main speaker that day, or his two-hour oration.

Brevity makes good common sense, for sure. But it becomes imperative when you start to think about your audience's tolerance and capacity for information. We are all succumbing to "Twitter-brain": shrinking attention spans that result from and demand shorter and shorter messages.

A Closer Look at Attention Spans

There is considerable debate about attention spans and about the effects of the digital world and handheld devices. Interestingly enough, just a few decades ago, the debate focused on the effect that television was having on attention spans. Digital devices like smartphones and tablets are just the latest and greatest scapegoats. Whether they have or haven't contributed to diminishing attention spans, it is certainly mind-boggling to realize that, with Twitter, full-bodied messages can be delivered in 140 characters or less.

The change in attention spans is often discussed in negative terms, as a deterioration in our ability to focus. But I think we have to ask ourselves, is this really a bad thing? I prefer to look at the phenomenon as a market disruption or correction that is forcing communications to adopt the often-touted corporate principles of leanness and efficiency. As companies try to increase engagement and productivity, improving communication—by cutting out waste—could be quite effective. Being brief and to the point may require a little extra effort, but it can accomplish a lot and save precious time.

Many studies have now measured adult attention spans—where they are and how they've changed over the years. There are reports suggesting that in just the last decade, the average adult attention span has shrunk from highs of twelve to eighteen minutes and to lows of three to five minutes, depending on the study's focus and the environments of the participants. Some studies look at how long people can concentrate on a task; others look at their attentiveness while listening. Yet how long people can pay attention to a speaker depends on tremendous variables that can make it hard to measure: the comfort and conduciveness of the environment, the speaker's voice quality and modulation, the actual content, whether there are effective visuals or good stories, what the objective is for the audience, and whether they understand that objective. The ability to focus is, after all, crucial to the achievement of an objective, so audience motivation levels can vary as well.

In addition, there are two types of attention: "transient attention," which refers to a short-term stimulus that attracts or distracts attention; and "focused attention," which refers to the attention given to a task or a speaker. Transient attention comes out pretty consistently at eight seconds, and we'll address this a little later in the chapter. Focused attention is where much of the debate lies and is the type for which experts claim that attention spans are as short as five minutes and as long as twenty.

Because of my own experiences and those of my clients, I gravitate toward data that measure and track attention spans in the workplace. When you think about it, most business meetings and presentations involve a sharing of information or a transferring of knowledge; the objective is that the people in the room will understand what they're expected to do, or that they will be able to make a decision.

According to research conducted by psychologist Dianne Dukette and physician David Cornish, adults are able to maintain twenty minutes of sustained attention. However, within those twenty minutes, the audience needs to experience a "stimulus change" every few seconds in order to maintain focus.[26] The stimulus change can be as subtle as the speaker moving or shifting positions or as overt as a change in visuals or sound. For the workplace, Dukette and Cornish's research boils down to three rules of thumb:

1. You have eight seconds to grab your audience's attention when you open.
2. You have a maximum of twenty minutes to transfer information.
3. You should "change things up" every few seconds during the interaction.

My experience suggests both that the researchers are right on target and that there are two significant challenges to following their advice. The first is that holding the attention of an adult audience requires a tremendous amount of multitasking. The second is that it requires careful advance planning.

In other words, brevity—or perhaps we should call it efficiency and expediency—in communication takes discipline and planning.

As the speaker, it's up to you to do the hard work of organizing your thoughts and packaging your content for your audience.

It's up to you to identify what you want your audience's takeaway to be and then deliver that. It's also your job to think ahead about your audience's experience and their appetite, or lack of appetite, for detail. Most of all, it's up to you not to get carried away and keep on talking just because you can. Being brief takes effort and discipline, but the end result—measured by the audience's impression of you and their retention of your message—will be well worth it. It's the effort and discipline of an all-star.

When someone speaks briefly, yet with the clarity, directness, and simplicity of Doc Rivers, the message sticks. He captured—and we got—an entire season's worth of game strategy in one word: "defense." Being able to drill down to the core and deliver a to-the-point answer like Rivers did requires both focus and discipline. The focus calls on factors of time, place, and audience. In this case, the time is a media interview, the place is the championship game, and the audience is composed of jubilant fans who want it straight and fast.

The discipline lies in remembering that it's not all about you, the speaker; discipline means saying to yourself, "Yep, sure I could go on for hours on this topic, but the time, place, and audience don't call for it and probably can't tolerate it." The discipline is reminding yourself that just because you have the floor doesn't mean you necessarily have the latitude to stay there. The result of brevity is that both you and your message are memorable.

One really easy and effective technique for keeping yourself on a diet of short and sweet is to think about talking less and engaging more, making your presentations more of a give and take. For example, make a point and then open up the floor for questions or discussion. Besides creating a change in stimulus, this gives you two other advantages: It provides you with feedback on your audience's level of understanding and buy-in; and it gives you insight into their biases and self-interests, both of which you need to know to achieve your desired outcome. I often encourage clients to use this technique when they've been asked to speak for an hour. Knowing full well that an audience can hang in there for maybe twenty minutes at a time, I encourage people to switch it up and take a Q & A break after each topic section of their presentation, rather than saving audience comments and questions for the end.

Another way to enforce brevity on yourself is to be a minimalist in your preparation. By that, I mean limit your written preparation to some simple bullet points. Once you get involved in writing a script for yourself, you become more and more wedded to the actual words you've written and the detail you've fleshed out in your script. I have found that some people need to start with a full-text script for their preparation and then work their way down to bullet points, once they're comfortable enough and familiar enough with the direction and content of their talk. That's great, too.

Ultimately, if you walk into a room with just the bullet points, you'll be less attached to the beautiful words and sentences you wrote and you'll be able to be more present with your audience. This is not to say that there aren't times that call for a full-text script; there may well be. But be aware that a script can shift you and your attention more to delivering what's on the paper than to connecting with the audience.

In the case of LeBron James's 2010 announcement, he simply took far too long to get to the point. Probably following the advice of agents or greedy TV executives, he played along with the idea of creating an event rather than making a simple announcement. In doing so, he lost sight of the fact that his audience was waiting, practically dying of curiosity, to hear what he'd do. Instead of winning his audience over, he frustrated them by dragging it out.

Four years later, when he delivered cogent comments, they

were reported and retweeted to an audience that suddenly seemed unable to get enough.

There's another pitfall besides not considering the audience's experience: assuming the audience has a bottomless appetite for detail. It's not just a matter of a shrinking attention span; there really is such a thing as too much information.

Here's another tip: When you need to make a point or deliver information, package it by giving the conclusion first, adding supporting information next, and then reinforcing it with the conclusion again. That conclusion, or summary statement, offers context for the supporting information, and it also captures the significance or value of the information to the audience. These statements are messages, and you can learn more about how to create and use messages and information in the final chapter of this book.

There's a reason why phrases like "the bottom line is," "at the end of the day," and "in a nutshell" are so commonly used: they work. Not only do they signal the coming of a summary statement, but they also shortcut the whole talk and make the material digestible for the audience. Messages become memorable, and information becomes dispensable, if necessary . . . for the sake of brevity.

Consider this quote from Muhammad Ali, who was talking about being a boxer: "It's just a job. Grass grows, birds fly, waves pound the sand. I beat people up." Brief, simple, impactful, to the point, and certainly memorable.

Brevity is one of the most important factors within your control as a speaker. It's a great tool and an attention-getter. It is memorable and, when used well, it is like a punt play: It gets the right result quickly.

Punt Play

1. **With brevity, everyone wins.** The speaker gets to the point and is therefore off the hook faster; the audience is always grateful.

2. **Less is more.** It's much easier for your audience to remember what you said if you're brief and succinct.

3. **To grab and hold attention, brevity is the perfect tool.** It can take a bit more planning and forethought to be brief, but it can have great impact!

Practice Exercise

Look at a talk or presentation that you recently gave. How long is it? In minutes, pages, or number of slides? What were the main points?

_____

_____

_____

_____

_____

_____

_____

Can you think of ways to shorten it or tighten it so that it's half as long?

_____

_____

_____

_____

_____

_____

_____

_____

Can you break it up by taking questions from the audience? Where and how would you do that?

_____
_____
_____
_____
_____
_____
_____
_____
_____
_____
_____

Finally, can you reduce the presentation to bullet points?

_____
_____
_____
_____
_____
_____
_____
_____
_____
_____
_____
_____

CHAPTER 6

TWO-A-DAYS

"Be prepared, no excuses."

In 2001 Josh Hamilton, who at twenty is one of Major League Baseball's most gifted, promising, and highly paid hitters, falls into drug addiction and off baseball's radar screen. Six years later he begins to work his way back, and by 2010 he is named the American League's MVP. On *Larry King Live*, Hamilton is asked the question on everyone's mind: "What happened?"

In his sincere, succinct explanation, Hamilton says, "You know, I was young, had the money, and just got caught up with the wrong crowd, and so I made some bad choices." The reality is probably a long story and not easy to explain, but the ballplayer is obviously prepared for the question—which he should be—and handles it like a pro.

Contrast Hamilton's ready response with Danica Patrick's post-race interview after her first major victory at the Indy Japan 300 in 2008—also the first-ever win for a female driver in American open-wheel racing.

Patrick is asked by an ESPN reporter what this historic victory means to her "personally and professionally." She answers:

"Well it's going to kick things up a notch, probably; you know, my first year in Indy was one phase of it and you know, I think that myself and a lot of us know that winning it was going to be the next phase, so um, you know, I'll probably be pretty busy for awhile, um, you know, definitely going to you know, be a lot more excitement personally probably, hopefully. *Hopefully.*"

Despite knowing the significance of a win, Patrick is completely unprepared; the interview is one of the longest, most rambling, and far-off-the-mark answers ever given in an historic moment.

Not unlike Tiger Woods's press conference, Josh Hamilton's comeback interview and Danica Patrick's historic victory ramblings are rare career make-or-break opportunities at the microphone. While Woods's over-preparation didn't overtly do additional damage, he didn't do himself any favors, either. Like Woods, Hamilton knew he had some reputational ground to recapture, and so he was prepared for his moment. But compared to Woods, Hamilton was less stiff, more authentic, and therefore more sympathetic. Patrick's lack of preparation was simply a missed opportunity; she failed to make the most of a moment that was bound to come.

While "two-a-days" might conjure up images of intense physical practice, the kind of preparation I'm suggesting is mental. It can take as little time as a minute, but if you can give it longer, great!

Being prepared is just about the most audience-centric thing you can do. It confers a sense of importance and value on your listeners. It shows respect for their time and is arguably the least you can do in exchange for their attentiveness to you as a speaker. Plus, it ensures that what you deliver is actually received. Preparation shows—as does a lack of preparation.

All too often, though, people resist preparing for a talk or a media interview. Clients have told me it feels egotistical or self-important to them, and they feel—or want to appear—more humble than that. In their minds, preparing a "speech"—whether that means welcoming remarks at an event, a thank-you for an award, or even an introduction for a speaker—feels bloated and unnecessary. Still, the principle from the first chapter of this book applies: "It's all about them—it's not about you!" You have a responsibility to deliver something of value to your audience, and the best way to do that is to be prepared.

When a speaker or presenter is prepared, the audience notices. The speaker is on point, and the message is clear and relevant to the audience. The prepared speaker doesn't open with, "Well, I didn't have time to prepare anything, so I hope you'll bear with me." Instead, the prepared speaker opens with an anecdote or an attention-grabbing factoid specific to that particular audience. Or the prepared speaker knows his or her desired outcome and puts it out there right up front.

There are many who speak or present in front of groups often enough that they feel it's okay—and in fact, for some it feels more comfortable—to just "wing it." Wingers are gamblers. Sometimes they win, but other times they lose. Since the outcome can go either way, you have to ask yourself if you can afford a loss. Or can you afford even to risk it? If speech prep were short enough and simple enough, would you devote just a few seconds to being prepared? I think anyone would.

It appeared as though Danica Patrick winged it when she won

the Indy Japan 300, and she didn't make the best impression at that particular moment. Maybe she wasn't expecting the victory that day, but she certainly was expecting it sometime. That's the interesting thing about sports and business; there are usually only two potential outcomes, a win or a loss (or success or failure). Part of preparation, then, is knowing how you would want to address each one.

Famed University of Alabama football coach Paul "Bear" Bryant said, "It's not the will to win that matters—everyone has that. It's the will to prepare that matters." It can be a differentiator, for sure.

So here are a few simple preparation tips that not only reduce your risk but actually connect you more quickly and directly with your audience.

Develop mini stump speeches. If you know there are projects or issues that you typically need to address, take a few minutes and develop some ready message points. These should be short, crisp statements that convey value or importance, focusing on the "why" and not the "what." If you have these in your back pocket and you're called on to speak, you're halfway there. Add a story or anecdote that illustrates your message, and you're good to go!

I worked with an organization where the CEO was planning to retire and a successor had been named, but there were still another twelve months until the transition would be complete. The retiring CEO had made quite a name for himself, and the organization was the object of a lot of public attention. As a practical matter, the CEO needed to prepare himself with a basic stump speech for all the media interviews he would be asked to give during his final year, as well as for all the business groups that wanted him to speak during those twelve months. We sat down for a morning, used a lot of giant sticky notes, and prepped a set of messages to be used in media interviews. We also shaped these into a basic stump speech for the talks he was invited to give. (This would be customized for specific occasions and audiences, of course.) In addition to the benefit of being ready at all times, the preparation we did together ensured that he delivered a strong and consistent career narrative, which became the story of his legacy.

Be selective with information. Whatever you do, don't fall into the trap of thinking if you just do a lot of research, present a lot of data, or share a lot of detail, that you're prepared to address an audience. Preparation requires you to think about the significance of your talk—the "why," not the "what"—and to be prepared to convey that before you get to any supporting information. Use your data or details to reinforce your point, not to make it or replace it.

Disrupt chronology. If you have only a few seconds or minutes to prepare, think about what your summary or conclusion would be for your talk—and then deliver that as your whole talk. If you feel the need to elaborate a bit more, at the very least use your summary as your opening. Disrupting chronology works because, as we've noted, the first eight seconds are when you have the highest level of attention from your audience. You might as well give them the bottom line right up front, while they're with you. And it doesn't hurt to reinforce your point again in your closing.

Even with these tips in mind, there are still barriers to preparation. There's the triple threat of fear, dread, and procrastination. There's also the brain paralysis that comes with not knowing where to begin and the physical paralysis that comes with being nervous about getting up to speak. Plenty of leaders suffer from any or all of these, but they fake it, mask it, or just plow through it.

Breaking the Paralysis: Where to Begin

Don't know where to begin? That can be solved by doing what I call "going up to 30,000 feet and looking down." Take the biggest-picture view you can find on your topic and be thought-provoking about what's at the core of your issue, or, as President George H. W. Bush is known to have called it, find that "vision thing." The view from 30,000 feet is the exact opposite of peering through the weeds, and while most people in an organization are by definition, and indeed by assignment, stuck in the day-to-day weeds, certainly a leader is in a position—and arguably has the responsibility—to rise to a higher vantage point.

For an example of a 30,000-foot view, let's look at another of my clients, an entrepreneurial company that manufactures super-high-end sports equipment. The executives came to me for spokesperson training in advance of what they expected to be a busy season of trade shows and competitions where their products and sponsored athletes would attract a lot of attention. The engineering and technology that goes into the production of their equipment is as fascinating as it is dense with detail and data. Yet for the media—and for the benefit of building and promoting the brand—they needed to develop some higher-level messaging. The nitty-gritty details could be saved for the trade journals that craved them.

In a small-group session with the core executive team, I asked a series of questions to elicit the 30,000-foot view. Fundamentally,

I was pushing and poking at them to home in and identify what their company is really all about. It's not about the product line or producing the best equipment; it's not about being made in America; it's not even about satisfied customers. Those are all great attributes, but they're closer to the ground. What the 30,000-foot exercise yielded in the end was that their company is all about three things, characterized in a different way: innovation, performance, and fun.

Having a 30,000-foot view of your organization's work in your back pocket means you're always prepared to speak at the higher visionary level befitting a leader. It gives you a go-to point when you need to make remarks that describe your work and its value.

Breaking the Paralysis: Dealing with Nerves

Nerves are another story. There are numerous reasons why speaking in front of a group strikes fear in the hearts of otherwise confident, successful, and charismatic people—and then blocks their ability to prepare. And there are quite a few tools and tactics to address nerves, depending on what causes them. One source of nervousness that I have found somewhat universal is the fear of feeling humiliated.

Recently in my coaching practice, I worked with two high-profile individuals concurrently. One was in the healthcare field, and the other was an attorney and up-and-coming politician. When I met them, both had an infrequent but increasing number of speaking engagements, and both were paralyzed at the thought of going to a podium unless they had put in tremendous amounts of preparation and practice time. Yet time was a luxury; it was in short supply for both of these busy professionals.

When I dug deeper with each of them, it turned out that what hung them up and made preparation difficult was an almost fatalistic view that they were bound to fail, because they weren't going to know absolutely everything they needed to know on their topics. I find this is a pretty typical concern for speakers at any level of an organization or at any point in their careers. People are afraid they will be caught with their pants down, so to speak: that they will be seen as frauds or not smart enough. Yet both of these clients were extremely bright, accomplished, well-respected professionals.

There are two questions I ask clients who present these self-constructed hurdles:

1.   When you are in the audience and a speaker demonstrates that he or she knows a great deal about the topic but gets tripped up on one question, does that kill it for you? Do you judge the speaker to be a complete fraud or an idiot?

1.   Do you have any evidence—for example, feedback from peers, third-party evaluations, even media coverage—that suggests you have ever failed at the podium? Is there any objective evidence that you don't know what you're talking about when you get up to make some remarks or lead a meeting?

The answer to both questions for most people is "probably not." And the answer from both of my clients was "no." For these two individuals, the biggest challenge was to get them to stop having a dialogue with themselves about what the audience might be thinking of them and start thinking about how they might have a dialogue with the audience about the topic. It's all about the audience, anyway!

Fortunately, for these two clients and others, curiosity and inquiry are two of the hallmarks of a successful twenty-first century leader; they have replaced being all-knowing and authoritarian. This means a leader at the front of the room is free to say, "I don't know," or to solicit input from others, or to offer to find an answer he or she doesn't readily have. Being human is not only acceptable; it has become more appealing, something that makes a leader seem more accessible and real.

One of the greatest hockey players of all time, Gordie Howe, offered this sage advice: "I always tell kids, you have two eyes and one mouth. Keep two open and one closed. You never learn anything if you're the one talking." Leadership is gravitating toward those who are open to listening and learning, so it is increasingly acceptable—and more desirable—for a leader not to have all the answers.

Preparing for the Unknown

There is some skill, however, in managing an audience during the most unpredictable, free-form—and therefore potentially unnerving—portion of a meeting or presentation: question and answer time, the infamous Q & A. Often overlooked during preparation and also overlooked as a source of nerves, Q & A can be quite helpful to a speaker. This is a time when the audience members' "what's in it for me?" need comes oozing out. That's a good thing, since it's all about them. So Q & A may be your one true opportunity to satisfy your audience. When it's done well, this can be the most connecting and engaging portion of a meeting or presentation. For some speakers, though, the anticipation of Q & A can feel like preparing to navigate a minefield.

Why not think of Q & A as your defensive game, since you don't know and can't control exactly what's going to come at you? Legendary Boston Celtics Coach Red Auerbach once said, "Basketball is like war in that offensive weapons are developed first, and it always takes a while for the defense to catch up." He's right. You're in control of your own offense, and with preparation you'll execute well. But defense is harder; it has to play catch-up.

To that end, here are some tips to keep in mind while you're on defense and managing Q & A.

Pause. When you field a question, pause, collect your thoughts, and figure out where you want to go with your answer. Unless you have a clear and unwavering yes or no to offer, jumping in too quickly to begin your answer has some risks: namely that you'll ramble or that you'll get carried away and deliver a whole new presentation in answer to that one question.

Identify whether the question was a question or a soapbox speech. This is another reason the pause is helpful; you need a few seconds to decide whether you actually fielded a question or a speech. Many times when people raise their hands during Q & A it's because they're so eager to make their own views heard. Those don't need to be answered, per se. You can just say "Thank you for your perspective on that" and then move on to the next question.

Have your brain perform a "key word" search. Rather than getting all tangled up in the language or tone of someone's question—all too often, it can be negative or biased in a way that is not favorable to you—use your few seconds of pause time to listen for a key word or the theme of what the individual is asking you. Then you can use that word or theme as a springboard to your answer, allowing you to use your own, more positive and affirmative language. Try to reach for a message—a summary statement or a statement of value or benefit—first, and then backfill with any detailed information that might be necessary. In other words, disrupt chronology—offer a quick sound bite first and the supporting background second.

BYOQ—bring your own questions. As a final step in your preparation for leading an important meeting, making a presentation or speech, and for managing Q & A, you should develop a handful of questions that you could throw in if necessary; say, if the group goes silent. These questions would serve as good discussion starters. (For example: "I presented a timeline, but I'm interested to know—are there are obstacles you think we should consider?") Or they could be questions that might help move the dial closer to the outcome you're looking for. ("Is there anything about what you've heard today that would get in the way of your making this decision?") These questions might even allow you to introduce a side point that you had no time for during the structured portion of your remarks. ("One thing we didn't have time to cover—but that has some relevance here—is the need for subcontractors. Would it help if I talked about that for a minute or two?") Being armed with some questions of your own is part of your preparation.

One final note: Q & A is where all five communications principles merge. It's a great time to connect and put all the pieces together. Instead of thinking of Q & A as a minefield, think of it as an opportunity to be audience-centric, gracious, transparent, brief, and prepared. All five characteristics will serve you well in the dialogue that ensues during Q & A.

Without a doubt, speakers and presenters who are better prepared tend to be more comfortable at the front of the room. This is true even for people who aren't plagued by nerves. Unfortunately, advance preparation is not always possible and, for some, it's not easy.

My one final tip for preparation is this: When and if you're desperate—there's no prep time, no notice, and you need a Hail Mary pass to get up and start talking—ask yourself one question, then flip it around and make that your opening sentence.

The question is this: *What do I want these people to think, know, do, or feel when I'm done talking*? If you want them to feel motivated, then your opening is, "I'm going to talk to you about [topic], and I want you to leave here today feeling motivated." If you need them to complete a project a month ahead of schedule, then your opening is, "We're going to review where we are on [project] this morning, and I have a clear call to action for all of you, which is to figure out how we can save a month." If you want your audience to have one key takeaway, then your opening is, "If you leave here remembering only one thing from this evening's program, I want it to be this . . ."

What is my ideal outcome? What do I want these people to think, know, do, or feel? The answer to those questions is your best and fastest shortcut to a strong opening when you have no prep time. Because then, if you have to just run with it—to wing it—you've used your first eight seconds well, and you are likely to have planted exactly the context and expectation that you needed your audience to have right away.

Two-a-Days

1. **Think of every public speaking opportunity as a performance or clutch play.** You'll pull it off a lot better if you show up prepared and ready to really perform! Your audiences will notice and appreciate it, plus they'll leave with a better impression.

2. **Have a stump speech or some core messages in your back pocket that capture the essence of you, your project, your company, or your goals.** Don't allow yourself to be unnerved by what you perceive to be a lack of time or low level of knowledge. You can still prepare to deliver 100 percent. Comprehensiveness and thoroughness are not always the most worthy goals; connection with the audience is!

3. **Preparation shows.** And while it's best to prepare from start to finish, including being ready for Q & A, it doesn't need to be cumbersome. There are shortcuts. Knowing and articulating your desired outcome for a meeting or presentation is the quickest method.

Practice Exercises

Think about a topic or topics that someone is likely to ask you about in the near future. What are they?

_____

_____

_____

_____

_____

_____

_____

_____

_____

Will you soon take on a new responsibility and have to describe your aspirations for the project? Outline your thoughts.

_____

_____

_____

_____

_____

_____

_____

_____

_____

_____

_____

Can you anticipate the questions you might be asked? What are they?

_____
_____
_____
_____
_____
_____
_____
_____
_____
_____
_____

Can you sum up, clearly and concisely, what you are working on? How would you describe it?

_____
_____
_____
_____
_____
_____
_____
_____
_____
_____
_____
_____

Are you about to leave some job or project behind? Can you sum up your accomplishments or give an overview of that experience?

_____

_____

_____

_____

_____

_____

_____

_____

_____

Consider your last experience with Q & A. Was there some question that stumped you? Were you nervous? Surprised? What would you do differently?

_____

_____

_____

_____

_____

_____

_____

_____

_____

_____

_____

Think about a difficult question you've fielded, then pause, do a "key-word search" for the topic or theme, and see if you can come up with a message or summary statement that would be the first sentence of your answer.

_____

_____

_____

_____

_____

_____

_____

_____

_____

_____

_____

_____

_____

_____

_____

_____

_____

_____

_____

_____

_____

_____

_____

_____

CHAPTER 7

GAME FACE

"Bring it!"

I think self-awareness is probably the most important thing towards being a champion.

—Billie Jean King

Body language . . . Presence . . . How you carry yourself . . . Eye contact . . . What to do with your hands . . . Your body movement . . . Billie Jean is right. If you plan to be a champ at the podium or the front of the room, you will need to be at least somewhat self-aware. Know what your personal inclinations—and, yes, habits—are, and then employ some simple best practices, which are discussed in this chapter. Look at yourself as a work in progress; it's that way for most people, myself included. Self-awareness (as well as feedback from a few honest, caring friends and colleagues) will keep you moving in the right direction.

Body language—which for most people means posture and what to do with arms and legs—deserves a few words because it is nonverbal messaging. That's the reason it's important: It can reinforce your message if it's sincere and if it matches your words . . . and, arguably even more important, it can reinforce *you* as the messenger.

When it comes to helping you make an impact with an audience—whether it's big or small, when you're on camera or off—my coaching practice is heavily oriented to messaging and the organization of thoughts. I'd estimate that with the average client, I spend 70 to 80 percent of our time on nailing down content (audience-centricity, transparency, graciousness, and brevity take time!) and 20 to 30 percent on physical delivery issues.

I've found that most successful people already have a measure of confidence, charisma, and presence that got them to where they are and that will carry them through a trip to the podium. Where they get hung up—causing their confidence to wane, their charisma to dim, and their presence to shrink—is on content. *Is this what the audience will want? Is my opening strong? Will I sound like I know what I'm talking about? What if I have to look at my notes? Should I tell that joke at the beginning?* (Usually safer not to—just saying.) *Will anyone be able to follow along? What if I don't know the answer to a question?* These are all content-centered issues, and they can distract—and destroy—the performance of an otherwise poised professional. Content is key.

Nonetheless, how you comport and present yourself is pretty critical, too, and there are some simple best practices that can enhance your delivery. Call them reminders, ones that are meant not as a kick in the pants but as a reassuring pat on the back:

1. **First and foremost, *decide* that you're going to bring your best game, that you're going to own the room and enjoy your time with your audience.** Seriously, if you make a conscious decision ahead of time and set

it as your intention, it is more likely to happen. And it will be the standard you hold yourself to as you move through your time with your audience. You've done it many times for a job interview; you can do it for a speech or presentation!

2. **With your body overall and with your arms or hands specifically, think *forward, up, and out*.** Stand tall. Lean and reach toward your audience instead of slinking back, collapsing onto one elbow, or crossing your arms. Point your feet toward your audience and stand on the balls of your feet as if you were poised and ready to jump into their laps. Keep your palms open. Don't be afraid to open your arms and "embrace" your audience. Avoid pointing, but open-armed, open-handed, outstretched gesturing is fine.

3. **Use your *voice*.** Modulate your tone as a way of changing things up for the audience. As we saw in chapter 4, attention spans are short and demand regular stimulus changes. Try to speak louder, softer, faster, or slower as appropriate for different portions of your presentation. And pause. Pauses are good; your audience needs time to digest your ideas.

4. **Use the *room*.** If there's a podium, try to get out from behind it. And, if possible, move around the room. That, too, will stimulate attention, changing the scene a bit and keeping the audience alert. However . . .

5. **Don't pace, and be aware of any *fidgety habits*.** Remember what your third-grade teacher told you

the first time you stood up to give a book report: Stand up straight. Don't jingle or play with things in your pockets. Don't fuss with your hair. We all want to hear what you have to say.

6. **Make *eye contact*.** That's huge. And not just with one friendly face. Try to cover as many faces and as much of the room as you can. Do not be put off (and I hear this all the time) by that "one guy in the front who was glaring at me the whole time." One man's glare is another man's look of concentration. You never know, so don't be distracted by one face. Just keep on looking at everyone.

7. **Let your voice and facial expression *match your words*.** In a sense, this goes back to being transparent. If you say you're excited, sound and look excited. If you're sad, sound and look sad. This is where a lot of executives fall down. With too much preparation, they can seem a bit wooden when it actually comes time for the presentation. You can use a highlighter on your notes to emphasize points that call for a little emotion—and then emote!

8. **Finally, unless you're delivering bad news, *smile*.** Presentations, keynote addresses, sales, or even fundraising pitches . . . these are the times to look positive. A smile completely changes the way your audience perceives you, and—believe it or not—it helps you relax and enjoy what you're doing.

Game Face

1. **Focus more on being present with your audience than on physical delivery.** There's a reason you've gotten as far as you have, and you're probably doing just fine. Instead, decide to bring your game face and be sure your content is infused with the five principles.

2. **Make sure your voice and expression match your emotions, and, if possible, get out from behind the podium and move around the room.** Your listeners' attention span is short, and changing things up keeps them engaged.

3. **Make eye contact and smile.** These are terrific ways to connect with your audience, and, in the end (also the beginning and middle) it's all about them.

Practice Exercise

Pick a paragraph from a book or magazine and just read it straight through.

_____

_____

Try reading it a second time aloud, investing the words or sentences with a little emotion.

_____

_____

Read it again, this time heightening the emotion and also attempting to modulate your voice, louder or softer, faster or slower. Throw in a hand gesture or two.

_____

_____

Finally, stand up and read it with a smile. (You can thank me later for not suggesting "Casey at the Bat," the classic and lengthy poem about a baseball game written by Ernest Thayer in 1888. I have forced many a client to deliver it on camera and emote while doing so!)

_____

_____

_____

CHAPTER 8

GAME DAY

"Play ball!"

Charles Barkley once said, "I'm not a role model . . . just because I dunk a basketball doesn't mean I should raise your kids." (Or run your business!)

These athletes—love 'em or hate 'em—are not necessarily literal examples of what to do or what not to do when communicating. But they do provide cautionary tales. They illustrate, sometimes in the extreme, what works and what doesn't work.

I hope the insights in this book have helped you think about how to take your communication game to the next level. Embrace the spirit of the five key communication principles outlined in this book in your everyday business life, and you'll already be ahead of other players. Put the principles into practice, and you'll be able to give your audiences the impression that you're an all-star every time you speak.

That said, you may be thinking, *Okay, I get it. I should think about my audience, be open and transparent, be gracious, be brief, and be prepared—but how do I put together a presentation or my remarks for an event?*

A Coach's Chalk Talk

What you're about to get in this section is a recap of the five principles in the context of a practical application—that is, how to use audience-centricity, transparency, graciousness, brevity, and preparedness in real communications.

Do you have a talk coming up? Maybe you need to present to a client or you're preparing to lead an important meeting. Whether it's weeks, days, hours, or even minutes from now, this chapter will help you be ready!

Any good coach will give a "chalk talk" before a game, outlining the strategy and plays, and that's exactly what follows. I'll show you how to prepare your remarks using a simple framework that embraces the five principles of communication you just read about.

As any athlete would, you need to get in the right head space first. Let's start with some mental prep work—or, as a sports psychologist might say, let's use a little positive imagery and have you thinking like a winner before you even leave your desk.

Imagine . . .

Making It All about Them

You've probably been an audience member more times than you've been a speaker, so you actually know quite well what an audience member likes or doesn't like, can or can't tolerate, and what holds or loses an audience's attention. When you're the speaker, none of that changes. You want to perform and deliver as a speaker exactly the way you would like to receive as an audience member.

That's the first principle of being an effective communicator: It's all about them—it's not about you.

Keeping your topic in mind, think about your audience:

- Who are they (decision makers, influencers, colleagues, supporters, opponents)?
- What do they really care about? What keeps them up at night?
- Where are they in terms of knowledge, interest, biases, concerns, and expectations?
- Why are they in the room—by choice or by obligation?
- How can you grab their attention, make the moment memorable, and leave a good impression?

Ultimately, the answers to these questions will tell you:

- How much and what kind of information (for example, background, detail) you should share—high-level or more general—and whether it should address a particular interest or concern.
- How much time you should take. Obviously, you can take more time with an audience that is in the room by choice rather than obligation.
- Whether you should include a funny story, an element of surprise, or a big idea.
- Whether you need visuals, and what they should be (slides, video, white board).

These decisions will be driven by who your audience is, the occasion, your topic, and any other relevant issues.

Setting the Right Tone

Tone and approach are key elements of a leader's voice. Here's where you want to use some positive imagery, especially if you're prepping for a high-stakes or difficult talk, when the principles of transparency and graciousness can be enormously helpful.

Picture yourself being clear, direct, and open about your intentions, your desired outcome, or the news you're sharing. Being open and transparent will score huge points for credibility, trust, and respect.

Be gracious, especially about your competitors and especially in the face of criticism. Be accepting, positive, and openhearted. And move on. Be the big person. No one remembers anything that an angry, vengeful speaker says, but they do remember the person's tone. Likewise, they'll remember the graciousness you exhibit; it'll label you as a class act. When in doubt, ask yourself, "What would Lou Gehrig do?"

Keeping It Brief

No matter how much time you think you have, plan on less. No one will complain if you finish talking earlier than expected!

When conference planners invite you to speak for an hour, it's only because it's easier to book eight speakers per day than sixteen. No audience can really hang on for an hour; in fact, we know that adults can only digest material for a maximum of twenty minutes. Even when the last fifteen minutes are reserved for the Q & A, those first forty-five minutes are likely too long unless you are able to break up the time with Q & A throughout, videos, group discussions and exercises, or appealing visuals.

As we noted before, adult audiences also need a stimulus change to stay engaged. Without it, they zone out periodically. I recently led a group of female executives who met monthly to practice making different types of speeches and presentations, and they all admitted to zoning out at least once during each other's talks, which, by the way, were capped at three minutes!

Audience attention is sharpest at the beginning and the end of a speech or presentation, so that makes openings and closings vitally important. In the middle, where the meat is, is where the audience zones out. The point is that it matters how you organize your material and guide your audience. And if it's absolutely necessary to fill an hour-long time slot, be aware of about a fifteen-to-twenty minute attention span limit. Break up the talk into sections, and keep each of those as brief as possible. Switch things up at fifteen-to-twenty minute intervals as a way to restart the attention span clock: turn on the PowerPoint, turn it off, solicit Q & A at the end of each logical section of your talk, draw or write on a white board, show a video. Choreograph the time with your audience's experience in mind.

It's all about them, so make some judgment calls about what will best suit your audience, including the length and structure of your presentation.

Being Prepared

The only element of your talk that is usually fixed and non-negotiable is your topic. That's it. The rest—how you open and close, whether you use visuals and what kind, how much time you take, whether you share stories or include Q & A—is up for grabs. These judgment calls are part of your preparation.

In a perfect world, you would have time to sit, contemplate, organize your thoughts, assemble some great visuals, recall a few of your favorite anecdotes to share, and rehearse. You'd be comfortable, confident, and charming every time all eyes were on you and you were the speaker.

The reality is often a little different. Nerves may throw you; they come with you even when you're prepared. Therefore, part of your mental prep work is knowing and accepting a certain amount of nervousness (adrenaline, actually) and committing to paying less attention to yourself and your butterflies and more attention to your audience and your engagement with them.

If having time to prepare is a not an option at all, remember the shortcut I described in chapter 5: Think about your desired outcome. In other words, when you're done talking, what would you like your audience to think? What would you like them to know? What would you like them to do? Or how would you like them to feel? Identify your desired outcome—it's a directive, almost like a call to action, but it is not a restatement of your topic—and spell it out in your opening. I call this a focal point.

If you have zero time to prepare, take a few seconds to identify your focal point and deliver it right up front. That way, if you have to wing the rest of your talk, at least you will have been incredibly clear and commanding from the start. (More on focal points in a bit.)

Play by Play

Okay, so for game day, you need to have some plays, right? I'm going to give you a five-part framework that makes writing your speech as simple as filling in the blanks—well, almost!

Here's what it would look like in a play by play, as if we were going to write it out on a chalkboard:

1. **Focal point / Opening**
2. **Message 1**
   Info for message 1
3. **Message 2**
   Info for message 2
4. **Message 3**
   Info for message 3
5. **Closing / Focal point**

Focal Point

In one sentence, you should be able to tell your audience what you want them to think, know, do, or feel when they leave the room. Your topic and your focal point are not one and the same; the focal point is your desired outcome.

Your focal point is always part of your opening and closing. It can even stand alone as your entire opening or closing. It sets a context and expectations for your audience so they don't leave the room and say, "That was interesting, but I'm not sure I get why I was in there."

Focal points start with phrases such as:

"If there is one thing I want you to remember today, it's . . ."

"By the time I finish this presentation, I know you'll be convinced that we're the right team . . ."

"My goal tonight is to inspire you, to get you more involved . . ."

You need to spell out your focal point. This is another place where transparency is key. Don't dance around what you want, and don't assume your audience will have the takeaway you hoped they would! Spell it out. Spoon-feed it.

Opening

Your opening can be as simple as a statement about your topic plus your focal point. Or it can include other modular pieces, such as a story or anecdote; an opening question to pique curiosity and build suspense; or an attention-grabbing factoid. Some of the best openings focus squarely on the audience—for example, recognizing the significance of their work or a recent accomplishment—but that's no big surprise. We already know it's all about them!

When you open, remember the lessons about transparency from chapter 2. If you need to issue an apology, start with an apology. If you have something to announce, announce it. If there's an elephant in the room—a recent crisis, a bad news story, the departure of a key executive—address it in your opening. It's a distraction if you wait or if you say nothing at all.

Keep in mind that audiences size you up and decide whether you're worth listening to in the first eight seconds, so use that time wisely. You can deduce from this that lots of pleasantries and niceties in your opening may not make the cut. If you absolutely have to include them, you might want to keep them super short or save them for the end (of either the opening or the talk itself). No matter what, though, you should include a focal point in your opening.

Messages

These are the building blocks of the body of your speech or presentation. They are the main points or thematic statements of your talk; they communicate significance, value, or benefit when you're being persuasive. They can also be conclusion or summary statements when you're being informative. Either way, they provide the context for any background information or detail that you want or need to share. If you were writing an essay, they'd be the concluding statements. So think about flipping standard chronology and opening each section of your talk with a message first and then backfilling with information. Think of it this way: conclusion first, followed by the evidence.

Being able to identify and articulate key messages is a huge help not only to the audience trying to follow along but also to you. If your time has been cut down significantly, you can go straight to messages and skip information, or you can prioritize and pare down the information you share. Knowing your messages also helps you visualize the sections of your presentation, so you're less dependent on notes or a script. Any slides you might create should be organized accordingly.

Just remember: no more than three key messages. You'll be lucky if your audience remembers one or two of them, let alone the third!

Information

Information is all the background, detail, data, statistics, stories, or examples that back up and support a message.

Information is important, but you have to choose it based on your audience (their level of interest, expertise on the topic, and so on). Remember, you can't share all your information. Pick and choose carefully. You must prioritize. Too much information is presentation buzzkill—but you already know this from your own experience as an audience member.

Word to the wise: Audiences don't connect their own dots, so a big data dump probably won't get them to the conclusion that's in your head. Connect the dots for them by having key message points that summarize or convey the significance or value of all your information.

Closing

In your closing, loop back to the opening. Echo your focal point and recap key message points. This is the time for phrases such as:

"Here's what I'm asking . . ."

"What it all comes down to is . . ."

"When you think of our organization, I want you to remember this one thing . . ."

These are clues that help alert your audience to listen up! And they give you a final opportunity to spoon-feed your audience what you want them to think, know, do, or feel.

Again, audience attention and retention levels are highest at the beginning and end of any speech or presentation. This makes openings and closings critically important, as they may well be the only parts of your speech that an audience remembers. So, following my own advice, here's the framework one more time:

1. **Focal point / Opening**

2. **Message 1**
   Info for message 1

3. **Message 2**
   Info for message 2

4. **Message 3**
   Info for message 3

5. **Closing / Focal point**

The Ultimate Takeaway: Game Day

If you take nothing else away from this chapter—or this book—remember the first principle of being an effective communicator: "It's all about them—it's not about you!" That's the reason I developed this framework. It's a best-practice model for capturing and holding an audience's attention (as much as you can!) and for building in moments for retention.

Practice Exercises

Be your own coach. Look at yourself as objectively as you can, and identify which of the five principles you need to work on the most. Which is it?

_____

_____

_____

_____

_____

_____

_____

_____

List the others in order of weakest to strongest.

_____

_____

_____

_____

_____

_____

_____

_____

_____

_____

_____

Work one "muscle group" at a time, beginning with your weakest. Identify at least one goal for each principle and how you might begin to achieve it.

_____

_____

_____

_____

_____

_____

_____

_____

_____

_____

Reinforce what you've learned. Pick your three favorite take-away tips from this book, and write them down.

_____

_____

_____

_____

_____

_____

_____

_____

_____

_____

_____

_____

Now transfer them to a note card, seal the card in a self-addressed stamped envelope, and ask a friend or colleague to mail it to you in three weeks. Getting the card in the mail is a great reminder to use the principles you learned!

_____

_____

_____

Now, once again, take a few minutes to search for a recent talk or two that you gave. Make a note of what you might have done differently, or better, based on the five principles in *Jock Talk*.

_____

_____

_____

_____

_____

_____

_____

_____

_____

_____

_____

_____

_____

_____

NOTES

Indroduction

1. Reed, Ted, "Delta, Up 78% This Year, Remains 'King of the Jungle,' Analyst Says." *The Street*, December 12, 2014.

2. Silverman, Rachel Emma, "Where's the Boss? Trapped in a Meeting." *Wall Street Journal*, February 14, 2012.

3. Einwiller, Sabine A., and Michael Boenigk (2012), "Examining the link between integrated communication management and communication effectiveness in medium-sized enterprises," *Journal of Marketing Communications*, 18, no. 5, 335-361.

4. Parks, Bob, "Death to PowerPoint!" *Bloomberg Business Week*, August 30, 2012.

5. Tufte, Edward R., *The Cognitive Style of PowerPoint: Pitching Out Corrupts Within*, Second Edition.

Chapter 3: Squaring to Bunt

6. Bob Nightengale, "Giambi: Baseball's Apology Needed over Steroid Issue," *USA Today*, May 23, 2007.

7. Dave Zirin, "Jason Giambi, Truthteller," *The Nation*, June 11, 2007.

8. Transcript of Tiger Woods press conference, February 19, 2010, http://www.nytimes.com/2010/02/20/sports/golf/20woodsstatement.html.

9. "Trust in Government," http://www.gallup.com/poll/5392/Trust-Government.aspx.

10. "2014 Edelman Trust Barometer," Annual Global Study, http://www.edelman.com/insights/intellectual-property/2014-edelman-trust-barometer/about-trust/.

11. Associated Press, "Selig Says Not Disciplining Giambi Was 'Appropriate Decision,'" ESPN.com, August 16, 2007, http://sports.espn.go.com/mlb/news/story?id=2977294.

12. Teri Thompson, Michael O'Keeffe, Christian Red, Nathaniel Vinton, "Alex Rodriguez Gets SLAMMED! Arbitrator Hits Yankees Slugger with Full-Season Ban, Plus Postseason," *New York Daily News*, January 11, 2014.

13. Romesh Ratnesar and Bill Saporito, "Tiger's Apology: A *Time* Discussion," February 19, 2010, http://content.time.com/time/nation/article/0,8599,1966761,00.html.

14. Timothy Coombs, quoted on Time.com, February 19, 2010, http://content.time.com/time/nation/article/0,8599,1966763,00.html.

15. Harvard Business School Centennial Summit, "Leadership for the 21st Century." October 13, 2008, http://www.hbs.edu/centennial/businesssummit/leadership/leadership-for-the-21st-century.html.

16. Written Testimony of General Motors Chief Executive Officer Mary Barra before the House Committee on Energy and Commerce Subcommittee on Oversight and Investigations, "The GM Ignition Switch Recall: Why Did It Take So Long?" April 1, 2014, http://media.gm.com/media/us/en/gm/news.detail

.html/content/Pages/news/us/en/2014/mar/0331-barra-written
-testimony.html.

Chapter 4: Alley-oop

17. William Rhoden, "Cleveland's Venom Validates James's Exit," *The New York Times*, July 9, 2010.

18. Diana Nyad, "Never, Ever Give Up," TedWomen 2013, December 2013, http://www.ted.com/talks/diana_nyad_never_ever_give_up.

19. David Garcia, Antonios Garas, and Frank Schweitzer, "Positive Words Carry Less Information than Negative Words," *EPJ Data Science*, May 18, 2012, http://www.epjdatascience.com /content/1/1/3.

20. Thomas Moore, "The Fight to Save Tylenol," *Fortune*, November 29, 1982, http://fortune.com/2012/10/07/the-fight-to-save-tylenol-fortune-1982/.

21. "HBS Awards for Alumni Achievement 2003—James E. Burke, HBS MBA 1949," Working Knowledge for Business Leaders Archive, Harvard Business School, October 27, 2003.

22. Jessica Duranda, "BP's Tony Hayward: 'I'd like my life back,'" *USA Today*, June 1, 2010.

23. Leigh Buchanan, "Between Venus and Mars: 7 Traits of True Leaders," *Inc. Magazine*, June 2013.

Chapter 5: Punt Play

24. LeBron James (as told to Lee Jenkins), "I'm Coming Home," *Sports Illustrated*, updated July 12, 2014, http://www.si.com/ nba/2014/07/11/lebron-james-cleveland-cavaliers.

25. Laken Litman, "Twitter Is Going Nuts about LeBron Going Home to Cleveland," *USA Today Sports*, July 11, 2014,

http://ftw.usatoday.com/2014/07/twitter-lebron-james-home
-cleveland.

26. Kaliym Islam, "Attention Span and Performance Improvement,"
Training Industry Blog, March 1, 2013, https://www
.trainingindustry.com/blog/blog-entries/attention-span-and
-performance-improvement.aspx.

ACKNOWLEDGMENTS

My gratitude and thanks go to many people. To Skip Everett, who first planted the suggestion that I write a book, and to Josh Sens, who interviewed the idea for *Jock Talk* out of me. To Emily Moench, who helped birth the first manuscript and query letter. To Sam Goldsmith, who helped identify and vet athlete stories. To Amber Sawaya, Kira Griffin, and Karen Kaminski, who sweated it out with me on an early version of this book. To Katie Eldridge, who provided me with a much-needed hideaway for endless days of writing so I could complete the manuscript. To Nelson Mills, who came in toward the end but whose help was invaluable. To the savvy folks at Greenleaf Book Group, who assigned me to two extremely talented editors—Carolyn Roark and Joan Tapper—both of whom coaxed and coached the *Jock Talk* manuscript from amateur to professional status.

A special shout-out to my board of directors, Janet, Annie, and Anne, for your encouragement, ideas, and loyal support since day one of SmartMouth, and to my colleagues in the Rutherford Group, five wonderful women whose individual and collective star power motivate me to go big but stay real. Heartfelt appreciation goes to the many dear friends, trusted colleagues, and admired clients who have supported me, SmartMouth, and *Jock Talk* through our various evolutions.

My humble thanks and abundant love to Nate, Hannah, and Molly Levine, who inspire and doubt me in equal measure, thereby raising the bar every day!

And finally, a nod to my brothers, David, Eddie, and Peter, who instilled in me early on that, as a girl, I would be useless in this world without at least some command of sports trivia.

ABOUT THE AUTHOR

 **Communications coach Beth Noymer** Levine is an expert in helping Fortune 500 executives, professional and world class athletes, and other high-profile individuals effectively think about, prepare for, and deliver their messages to important audiences. She is known for her rapport with her clients, her quick understanding of their business and communications challenges, and her emphasis on speeches and presentations that work for both the audience and the speaker.

The founder of SmartMouth Communications (www.smartmouthgroup.com), Levine has more than twenty-five years' experience in public relations and communications and has worked on both the agency and corporate sides, in New York and Atlanta. She currently maintains an office in Salt Lake City and an active presence on both coasts. Levine has written speeches, developed messaging strategies, and coached business executives, politicians, other professionals, and, notably, athletes.

Her clients have included members of the Utah Jazz, the US Ski Team, US Snowboarding, the US Speedskating Team, and several collegiate athletes.

A native of Boston, Levine has a degree in economics from Franklin & Marshall College, has completed a post-MBA program at the Tuck School of Business at Dartmouth, and holds certificates in training and in coaching from the American Society for Training and Development. She is also the creator of the "SmartMouth Public Speaking Toolkit," a five-star-rated mobile app for iOS devices available in the iTunes store (app.lk/smartmouth). Levine has lectured at New York University, the University of Utah, and the Tuck School of Business, and is in frequent demand as a speaker and workshop leader.

She is forever trying to hone the messaging for her toughest clients—her three children, Nate, Hannah, and Molly.